RIO GRANDE
HIGH STYLE
FURNITURE CRAFTSMEN

RIO GRANDE

HIGH STYLE

FURNITURE · Craftsmen

BY ELMO BACA

GIBBS·SMITH

PUBLISHER

97 96 95   5 4 3 2 1

This is a Peregrine Smith Book,
published by Gibbs Smith, Publisher
P.O. Box 667
Layton, Utah 84041

Designed by Traci O'Very Covey
Edited by Gail Yngve

About the Cover: Furniture in the cover photograph
designed by Doolings of Santa Fe, New Mexico; overstuffed chair designed by Nellie Barr Furniture.
Photographed near Santa Fe, New Mexico, at El Rancho
de las Golondrinas by David Marlowe. (Photograph
courtesy of Doolings of Santa Fe, New Mexico)

Printed in Hong Kong by ColorPrint Offset

Library of Congress Cataloging-in-Publication Data

Baca, Elmo.
Rio Grande high style: furniture craftsmen / by Elmo Baca
p. cm.
ISBN 0-87905-621-5
1. Furniture making—Southwestern States. 2. Interior
decoration—Southwestern States. 3. Interior decoration—
Southwestern States—Pictorial works. 4.
Cabinetmakers—Southwestern States. I. Title
TT194.B33 1995
749.218—dc20 94-37785
CIP

DEDICATED

TO THE

CARPINTEROS

OF OLD

NEW MEXICO

CONTENTS

INTRODUCTION

The landscape of Rio Grande country has inspired artists and designers for centuries, beginning with prehistoric Native American cultures. The natural splendor of the land and its great river continues to be an integral part of Rio Grande high style, as described by Mike Godwin, owner of Ernest Thompson Furniture of Albuquerque. "New Mexico is so visual; there's a lot of interesting colors and textures all around. I'll get ideas for new pieces just driving around and looking at the landscape."

▲ A group of Spanish Colonial benches in various states of disrepair were photographed in 1912 between the mountain villages of Trampas and Penasco in northern New Mexico. Benches such as these were made to serve as a family's church pew and also for seating in the home.
▼

Rio Grande country has also been witness to a startling pageant of history, which has included early Spanish explorations and subsequent colonization, the much anticipated opening of the West to American trade with the Santa Fe Trail after 1821, and the romantic pursuit of western paradise and adventure on Route 66.

At least five centuries of history and culture have combined to produce a tradition of furniture making in Rio Grande country that is at the same time primitive and complex, natural and painted, baroque and modern, delicate and massive, medieval and machine age. Rio Grande high style boasts no fewer than six stylistic movements, all developed by historical consequences and great craftsmen, and tempered by the available technology of their era.

Although nurtured by the oldest indigenous cultures, Native American-inspired furniture is among the most recent and contemporary of the Rio Grande styles. Many people are familiar with the Spanish style of Rio Grande country, now almost four centuries old, still vibrant and evolving. Rio Grande high style has also nurtured two popular and distinctly American furniture styles—the Cowboy/Ranch and the Mission, developed from the Arts and Crafts movement of a century ago. One of America's most charming furniture styles, Taos Country, captured the design world by storm several years ago. With roots in Taos' fabled art colony, Taos Country offers everyone whimsy and playful folk art designs. Even lovers of sophisticated modernist architecture and interior design will find a remarkable group of Contemporary Craftsmen in Rio Grande country, whose elegant furniture can grace a Santa Fe adobe villa or a sleek Madison Avenue penthouse.

Only today, however, are all six

The Meadows Hotel of Las Vegas, New Mexico, shown here about 1920, was an elaborate Mission Revival building with stylistic roots in California and Latin America. The Mission Revival style was popular from 1900 to 1930 in New Mexico.

movements of Rio Grande high style flourishing simultaneously. Rio Grande craftsmen freely borrow ideas from each other and also from the vast repertoire of superb historic examples that have preceded them. This spirit of cross-pollination and collaboration is one reason for the popular success of Rio Grande high style.

In the words of Ernest Thompson's Mike Godwin, "I also study the old (furniture) pieces and look for details that I like. We have so many influences to choose from here. For our Sandia (lounge) chair, I really liked the curve of a chair arm made in New Mexico in the nineteenth century that has a classical, Empire-style profile. So we refined it a little bit and expanded the proportions to modern dimensions. It's been a great seller for us."

Mike's wife, Doreen, adds that "one thing I really appreciate is the fact that New Mexico has a long tradition of furniture makers. Some places are richer

A photograph of the interior of the Taos home of famed scout Kit Carson shows a refined taste for eastern furnishings such as the Eastlake-style dining chairs. The Kit Carson house is now a popular museum located near the Taos Plaza.

in cabinet makers. But here, the craftsmen are trained to think in three dimensions, and the furniture has a wonderful, sculptural quality."

Just a generation after John Wayne and Gary Cooper personified western

ROMANCE OF THE WEST

style and values in classic Hollywood western movies of the 1950s and 1960s, and a century after the wild heydays of the Old West, western culture has once again captured the imagination of America.

The West is no longer the stereotyped frontier wilderness where men, women, and children struggle to survive against the cruel whims of nature or violent passions of lawless people and animals. Today, the West has evolved and matured into a major region of the world, practically a nation unto itself, possessing its unique history and culture, now proven to be eternal and captivating to millions of people.

Among the West's many art forms, furniture making has made spectacular

strides since 1975, capitalizing on the public's fascination with the frontier and country lifestyle. Much of western furniture's current vitality and original expression is being generated by a region generally defined as the watershed or drainage of the Rio Grande, a legendary river of history and adventure and home to many great craftsmen and artisans.

Because of its ancient association with Native American culture, believed to have begun about 15,000 years ago, and much more recently with Spanish tradition (over 400 years ago), the Rio Grande has produced a lifestyle and culture perhaps foreign to many people. Nowhere else in the New World has European culture blended so freely with the rich and bold colors, designs, textures, and raw materials of Native America than in Rio Grande country.

Paradoxically, the West (and also the Rio Grande) is home to some of America's pristine natural wilderness and also the most technologically advanced facilities for nuclear and high technology research in the world. Rio Grande high style furniture reflects this contrast, producing rustic-looking range furniture fashioned of salvaged forest wood, and also space-age refined, chair sculptures of polished steel that boast etched Native American petroglyph symbols.

Here, too, is the familiar cowboy-and-Indian style, well known to the world but now developing a sophisticated and appealing sense of design. Indian designs and craft techniques are now emerging on furniture and accessories, and cutting-edge designs are discovering a world of possible expression in leather, bone, beadwork, and textiles. Rio Grande cowboy furniture is borrowing techniques of tooled leather from saddlemakers and refining the timeless fashion of fringed leather and tanned suede to produce distinctive sofas and easy chairs.

The resurgence of the Rocky Mountain West after 1985 has produced a new generation of boomtowns and design centers. From the Thomas Molesworth-inspired, cowboy style of Cody, Wyoming, to the Hollywood glamor of Aspen and south to the artists' haven of Taos and the exotic Spanish and Indian stronghold of Santa Fe, the West is now basking in an unprecedented design and cultural renaissance.

This dynamism has revived the Spanish and Mission styles, now producing works of unparalleled carving virtuosity and refinement. Free exchanges and blending of design expression along tribal or ethnic lines from Mexico, Africa, and the Pacific

Northwest are now being manifest for the first time.

Some skilled craftsmen in Rio Grande country have pushed the horizon further; by fusing some classical styles such as Greek Revival, Chippendale, or German Biedermeier with western materials, artists have discovered yet another avenue for expression. Rio Grande high-style furniture in the 1990s can truly claim to have risen to a world-class status and appeal. With a broad-based and diverse set of stylistic movements—including Spanish, Native American, Mission, Taos Country, and Contemporary—Rio Grande high-style furniture is now a significant and original American art form.

From the high mountains of Southern Colorado to the balmy waters of the Gulf of Mexico, the Rio Grande has nourished a ruggedly beautiful land, perhaps best known as the homeland of the Pueblo Indians and their ancestors, the Anasazi, known as "the old ones." Near the great river's banks

The Curio Shop in the Alvarado Hotel, Albuquerque's great railroad hotel that was lost to the wrecking ball in 1970, displays many furnishings and crafts that became synonymous with the Mission style. This 1905 view shows the "new" Southwestern style, which was popular at the turn of the century.

RIO GRANDE COUNTRY

▲ A Spanish Colonial chest displays many of the well-known icons of New Mexican carving style, including rampant lions, central rosette, stylized pomegranate plants, and a scalloped border.

Snaking through volcanic mesas northward between two majestic mountain ranges, the Jemez and the Sangre de Cristo, the river was never far from the first Spanish settlements of San Gabriel, founded near the joining of the Rio Grande and the Rio Chama in 1598, or its successor, the first permanent capital of Santa Fe, founded in 1610. A second villa, Santa Cruz de la Canada, was settled in 1695.

From these first European communities along the Rio Grande, a new lifestyle emerged, demanding dedication, resourcefulness, and painstaking labor from the colonists for survival. The Spaniards relied on the ancient technology of constructing buildings with sunbaked mud bricks, known as adobe, learned from North African cultures. Adobe houses were especially well suited to the extreme temperature fluctuations and poor material resources of New Mexico.

and *bosques,* some of the earliest artifacts of man's presence in North America, remnants of Folsom Man and Sandia Man have been discovered.

Nearly five centuries ago, the river was forded by Spanish adventurers and colonists searching for treasure and the promise of a new beginning. North from the ruins of a shattered Aztec empire and the new imperial capital of Mexico City, these determined souls pressed on through the Jornada del Muerto, the Journey of the Dead, through the parched wastelands of northern Chihuahua and southern New Mexico, never venturing far from their lifeline of water.

From El Paso del Norte, an oasis in the northern Sierra Madre Mountains, the broad river climbs slowly through the high desert to a lush valley beneath the Sandia Mountains, where the villa of Albuquerque was founded in 1706. Here in the heartland of the young province of Nuevo Mexico, the river's waters were guided carefully into the fields and gardens of the struggling colonists and the neighboring Pueblo villages by ditch systems, called *acequias.*

Because of the extreme isolation of New Mexico, several months' journey overland from Mexico City, the material comforts of European homes were rare on the frontier, and common luxuries such as furniture were afforded by only a few wealthy families and dignitaries. In contrast to the English colonies, where fine furnishings arrived regularly in the emerging seaports of Boston, New York, and Charleston, Spanish colonists learned to improvise technologically and stylistically. The Spanish Colonial style of New Mexico, created in the seventeenth and eighteenth centuries, is the foundation for today's Rio Grande high style.

An unidentified New Mexican residence of about 1940 displays a pure and simplified interior style that presents both Spanish Colonial and Spanish Colonial Revival pieces. This blending of popular Spanish styles is a trademark of contemporary Rio Grande high style.

Many people would call New Mexico's Spanish Colonial furniture primitive or folk art because simple carpenter's tools were rare on the New Mexican frontier during the seventeenth and eighteenth centuries. Juan de Onate's colonial expedition of 1598 included several carpenters, who collectively boasted "six axes for cutting wood, two chisels, three adzes, one auger, and two thousand nails." According to Felipe Escalante, the entire expedition carried fifty-one axes, eight saws, nineteen augers, twelve chisels, eight adzes, one wagonmaker's hammer, two sets of compasses, and two planes. Forged metal, such as iron and brass for cabinet hardware, was also difficult to obtain in colonial New Mexico. Simple eyelet hinges made of bent nails were often used.

The scarcity of nails and glue

RIO GRANDE HIGH STYLE: THE SPANISH TRADITION

forced early *carpinteros* (carpenters) to use mortise-and-tenon joinery to construct their furniture. Most distinctive in New Mexican furniture is the use of the exposed wooden tenon that passes entirely through the board in which the mortise (or socket) is cut. The resulting exposed peg has become an expressive and decorative feature. Wooden dowels and wedges were also employed to strengthen the joinery. Other joinery techniques, such as dovetail joints (especially on chests) and the appearance of tongue-and-groove edges later in the nineteenth century, help characterize authentic New Mexican furniture.

The physical effort required to make pieces of furniture in colonial New Mexico explains their great value in their own day and in contemporary galleries. Trees were felled by ax or with the two-handed Spanish bucksaw, the *sierra.* Axes, adzes, and the smaller handsaw, or *serrucho,* were employed to create crude boards from the rough timber. Boards were adzed and planed by hand, since sandpaper could not be relied upon to smooth a board's finish. What resulted were chairs, tables, chests, and benches of unmistakable quality: crude and massive, yet often displaying inventive and charming details.

After Fray Andres Juarez introduced Spanish carpenters to Pecos Pueblo in the 1620s, native Pecos carpinteros became well known throughout the New Mexican colony for their excellent furniture. Unfortunately, much of this early seventeenth-century colonial furniture was destroyed during the Pueblo Revolt of 1680.

Pecos remained a cabinet-making center in New Mexico following the reconquest of 1692, but after 1700 the trade became diffused through various families and settlements. Spanish and Indian carpinteros were trained, and their knowledge and tools tended to be passed down through sons and sons-in-law, creating an unwritten, loosely structured, guild system. By 1790, there were forty-four carpinteros listed in the Spanish census, representing nearly every settlement in the colony.

As a result, until 1821, when New Mexico opened her markets to the Santa Fe Trail and also became a Mexican territory, the basic forms of New Mexican Spanish Colonial furniture changed very little. The furniture was commonly made of pine, while other woods such as cottonwood and red spruce were used for *santos* (religious figures) and some architectural details.

Most popular in the colonial New Mexican household was the *caja* (chest), for the simple reason that clothing and valuables could be stored there and kept safe under lock and key. A simple board chest was made

by joining four side boards together (usually by the use of a dovetail joint) and attaching the top and bottom by pegging or metal hinges. Another common chest style employed vertical legs or stiles to lift the wooden box off the ground.

Chests tended to display the most elaborate examples of carving, pictorial design, and painting in New Mexico Colonial furniture. Many of the design motifs, such as rosettes, pomegranates, lions, and crosses, are popular Spanish artistic inventions that originated in the Middle Ages. Renaissance and baroque stylistic inventions never reached isolated New Mexico. Other chests, largely from the Santa Cruz-Taos area, boast chip-carved designs in a *Mudejar* or Moorish style.

The humble origins of many of New Mexico's colonial families and the medieval residential habits of the Spanish help explain the relative scarcity of chairs and benches on the New Mexican frontier. Only wealthy families, clergy, and government officials could afford these luxuries. Tables were often made for use in the churches and appear quite small by modern standards. *Mesas redondas* (round tables) with chip-carved designs are distinctly New Mexican.

Common Spanish furniture motifs were combined in a new way in the 1930s to create a furniture style that may be described as Spanish Colonial Revival. The Regional Building conference room of the National Park Service in Santa Fe espoused this new Rio Grande style.

The priest's chair, or armchair, has become a popular collectible for many furniture aficionados. The ample proportions and ornamentation of the priest's chair bestow instant status to the sitter. The construction and stylistic origins are apparently derived from Romanesque thrones of the Middle Ages. In Mexico, this type of chair was known as *silla francesa* (French chair). The overwhelming majority of New Mexican colonists, however, sat on armless side chairs, stools, built-in adobe banquettes, or the hard-packed earth floor.

In a similar fashion, beds were unknown in Spanish colonial New Mexico. As late as 1846, according to Santa Fe Trail chronicler Susan Magoffin, people slept on wool sacks and sheep pelts. By day, the wool sacks were used as floor cushions, and sheep pelts were suspended from the ceiling.

Despite the spartan and humble nature of home furnishings in colonial New Mexico, the *trastero* (cupboard) became the principal piece of furniture and, for many, symbolizes New Mexico's unique furniture heritage. A great, upright cabinet, sometimes towering nearly seven feet in height, the trastero prototype has become the carpintero's principal means of creative expression. Sometimes these cabinets were hand painted with gesso and natural pigments. Later in the nineteenth century, intricately punched tin sheets were inserted into cabinet doors to create a pie-safe cabinet. Inventive carpenters also began to apply moldings and decorative motifs to cabinet panels for handsome relief effects.

Having become a symbol of New Mexico, the modern trastero is often a display of the carpintero's inventiveness, virtuosity, and wit. The latest fashion, perhaps influenced

New Mexico's Spanish Colonial Revival furniture was designed to adapt to modern uses such as this attractive dining buffet, photographed about 1935. The pleated carving ornamentation of this cabinet may be influenced by New Mexican tinwork.

by California taste, features boldly painted designs on the cabinet. Carved figures are carefully painted to heighten a relief effect, and new pictorial motifs such as flowers, birds, and assorted animals are being introduced. Other materials such as glass, metal, and exotic woods are being juxtaposed with pine, and similarly, a new variety of cabinet hardware is being explored for use. The trastero is increasingly being purchased as a freestanding work of art as well as for storage.

Another popular traditional form, the *banco* (bench) has also steadily evolved in form and ornamentation through the centuries. Originally, benches were manufactured for use as church pews by prosperous families but also were used to support swooning ladies at the fandangos, a typical example of New Mexican pragmatism. Adapted stylistically from the priest's chair, the bench has traditionally displayed pleasing proportions and

geometric designs. The modern use of paints, stains, and various finishes—often turquoise—has given the New Mexican bench a lighter, more playful spirit.

Other interesting Spanish Colonial furniture types included the *harinero* (grain chest), the *vargueño* (secretary), and the *taramita* (footstool). Recently, the *repisa* (wall shelf) has become a popular and simple motif for creative expression. The taramita and vargueño have virtually disappeared from New Mexico, while antique examples of the grain chest are the prized possessions of numerous Santa Fe-style collectors.

After the American annexation of New Mexico in 1846, local carpentry nearly abandoned the Spanish Colonial forms, becoming influenced instead by Eastern and European styles. New forms such as daybeds, writing desks, and bookshelves were first introduced into New Mexico by American army officers and merchants. Soon, native

New Mexicans began discarding their handmade furniture for manufactured pieces from the East. Because of Archbishop Jean Baptiste Lamy's influence, the handsome benches that served villagers as church seating were replaced by permanently installed pews.

New Mexican furniture of the latter half of the nineteenth century marks a radical departure from the Spanish Colonial style. Better tools became available, such as molding planes and lathes, and lumber mills began producing sawed lumber in various sizes and widths. Freed from board production, local carpinteros manufactured many more pieces much more economically. In 1860, four Santa Fe cabinet shops produced more than 1,500 pieces of furniture. Anglos and Hispanics alike boasted houses furnished in the latest Victorian fashion, often influenced by the English designer Charles Eastlake.

Out of this period of heavy Anglo-European influence (1850–1920), another unique New Mexican prototype, the Taos bed, was invented. With stylistic roots in the Craftsman and Mission styles of the early twentieth century, which were quite popular in California, the Taos bed has become recognized as a New Mexican classic. Similar to a nineteenth-century lounge, the Taos bed's versatility as a sofa, a sleeper, or lobby seating is a large part of its attraction for the contemporary buyer.

Powerful mercantile companies, such as Charles Ilfeld's in Las Vegas, New Mexico, quickly learned how to retail mass-produced furniture and use the railroads for easy shipping and warehousing. By 1925, the unique, handcrafted, New Mexican furniture of the eighteenth and nineteenth centuries had been virtually forgotten.

For carpinteros of the Rio Grande homeland, the new twentieth century promised the demise of traditional handcraftmanship and paradoxically its preservation and

TOWARDS THE TWENTIETH CENTURY

ultimate triumph. By World War I, modernism and the advent of a machine age had taken firm root in intellectual circles in Europe and the United States as technological advances seemed to be achieved daily. Early automobiles, airplanes, telephones, and moving pictures heralded a new age.

Not all designers were swayed by the machine aesthetic or the progress bestowed by the Industrial Revolution of the nineteenth century. Stylistic movements such as the Arts and Crafts and Art Nouveau emphasized natural forms and materials. In England, as early as 1836, Augustus Pugin championed a medieval guild system for craftsmen to foster a democratic society with high design standards and a high quality of life. Later, John Ruskin preached in his influential books *The Seven Lamps of Architecture* (1849)

and *The Stones of Venice* (1851) a return to original English and American design instead of an international machine aesthetic. Ruskin firmly believed that only if a piece of furniture was produced from beginning to end by the same man could high quality of product and work be achieved, a principle still present in many of the Southwest's furniture studios.

William Morris, an avid student of Ruskin's, established an English company by 1861 to produce furniture, stained glass, hardware, wallpaper, and other interior decorative products, stressing natural materials and designs. By 1888, the English Arts and Crafts Exhibition Society was formed, stressing functionalism, simplicity, and honest craftsmanship. These ideas would greatly influence the work of great American designers such as Frank Lloyd Wright and Gustav Stickley, as well as the Southwestern Mission style.

After the Civil War, both American and English home design had been radically transformed by wave after wave of Victorian revivals such as Queen Anne, Italianate, and Romanesque. Milled lumber, architectural elements and moldings, and manufactured furniture swept the frontier as well, creating entire Victorian boomtowns, from glamorous San Francisco to gritty mining towns across the West.

Reacting to the ostentatious display of ornament and materials characteristic of Victorian style, English writer Charles Lock Eastlake published his bestseller *Hints on Household Taste* in 1868, which was later published in the United States in 1872. Eastlake's book caused a design sensation on both sides of the Atlantic, offering broad advice on all elements of interior design, with the overarching suggestion towards functional, more simply designed furniture. Scores of Eastern manufacturers adapted Eastlake's ideas to produce Eastlake furniture, which quickly appeared in remote Southwestern railroad towns.

The philosophy of nineteenth-century English designers and writers concerning furniture was well suited to the actual traditional practice of New Mexico's carpinteros, who had no choice but to practice honest craftsmanship with available natural materials and tools. Cheap manufactured furniture, modern consumer tastes, imported styles, and other pressures at the turn of the century nearly caused the abandonment of the Spanish Colonial tradition.

Three broad philosophical and stylistic movements serve to create a framework by which contemporary Rio Grande furniture may be assessed in its development in the twentieth century: antimodernism, modernism, and postmodernism.

A REACTION TO MODERNISM

In their seminal book, *New Mexican Furniture 1600–1940,* Lonn Taylor and Dessa Bokides outline the influence of the antimodernist movement on the Spanish Colonial Revival between 1900 and 1940.

Several recent writers have defined and explored different aspects of antimodernism in the United States and Western Europe. Jackson Leers has seen it as the source of the turn-of-the-century interest in medieval, oriental, or other primitive cultures, of the pursuit of the strenuous life or of intense religious experience, and of the attempt to recreate a sense of economic and spiritual self-sufficiency throughout the Arts and Crafts movement. Kenneth Ames, focusing on the broader effects of antimodernism on attitudes toward the past, has written that "central elements in the response to modernism are orientation toward either preindustrial alterna-tives in the present, and emphasis on handicraft, and antiurban bias—which usually translates into an emphasis on rural life—and an inclination to stress simple rather than complex social structures, homogenous, cooperative folk rather than diverse, competitive people" (P. 213, New Mexico Furniture, Museum of New Mexico Press, Santa Fe, New Mexico).

The discovery of New Mexico by renowned artists, writers, and other intellectual lights at the turn of the century coincided perfectly with the search for primitivism, a rural lifestyle, and other antimodern sentiments. Still, surviving Native American cultures in the Southwest and a nearly perfectly preserved Hispanic-American culture in northern New Mexico provided these artists plenty of readily available subjects and themes for creative interpretation.

Early architectural projects in the new Pueblo Revival style were often based on historical prototypes. Architectural elements and carvings for the new Fine Arts Museum, created by Jesse Nusbaum, Kenneth Chapman, and Sam Huddleston, transformed traditional designs into modern proportions and more precise craftsmanship.

Furniture created for the museum was a synthesis of Spanish Colonial design motifs and Arts and Crafts styling and craftsmanship. Besides familiar tables, chairs, benches, and chests, the sideboard—an Eastern favorite—was introduced. Moorish chip-carving techniques and decorative forms such as the rosette became popular models for the new Spanish Colonial furniture.

The lobby of Albuquerque's historic La Posada, an early Hilton hotel, blends Spanish Colonial and Mission-style architecture and design.

Other threads of the tapestry we know today as Rio Grande high style also had their origins near the turn of the century. By 1900, after the West had been conquered, the buffalo slaughtered, and the Native Americans decimated, many Americans developed a sense of nostalgia for a vanishing lifestyle. Cowboy and western artifacts and memorabilia became highly collectible. The crafting of furniture out of discarded longhorns became a novelty, largely to satisfy the appetite of well-to-do eastern dandies who fancied a piece of the Old West in their living rooms.

THE BEGINNINGS OF RIO GRANDE HIGH STYLE

The Santa Fe Railroad developed an effective marketing campaign based on the mystique of the Southwest and access to "Indian Country" via motor detours from Las Vegas, Santa Fe, Albuquerque, and Gallup. Legendary restaurant and hotel accommodations, provided under the management of Fred Harvey, were offered in romantic theme hotels such as the Mission-style Castaneda in Las Vegas, the Alvarado in Albuquerque, the Pueblo Revival-style La Fonda in Santa Fe, or the Pueblo Deco-style El Navajo in Gallup. Architect Mary Colter designed and furnished the El Navajo in Gallup in an inspired eclectic approach, employing western fringed-leather sofas, wicker chairs, wrought-iron lamps in Pueblo cloud motifs, Navajo rugs, and even authentic, sandpainting-style designs on the walls.

After 1900, the California Mission style reigned in the Southwest. West Coast designers such as the Greene brothers and Irving Gill applied the values of the Arts and Crafts movement to California's historic Mission architecture and created a new, appealing architectural style. Arts and Crafts oak furniture was slightly modified by western craftsmen, allowing for minor Japanese and Spanish influences, and Mission-style furniture was introduced.

Mission-style champion Charles

F. Lummis adapted New Mexican Spanish Colonial motifs such as trastero panels to furniture designed for his Los Angeles house, El Alisal. Sophisticated joinery and finishing techniques created by Greene and Greene still influence several contemporary Mission craftsmen. The streamlined, modernist, Mission style of Irving Gill even included horsehide-bound side chairs that still appear contemporary in the 1990s.

Eclecticism based on Spanish, Mission, and Pueblo prototypes seemed to characterize the 1920s in the Southwest, a spirit not unlike today's. Various hybrid styles were invented, with strong romantic overtones, such as Spanish Gothic Revival, Pueblo Deco, and Mediterranean. These expressions appear to reflect the exuberance of the Jazz Age and also the new popular appeal of the West, Hollywood, and cultural stereotypes such as Cowboy and Native American themes. The design attitudes of stylistic revival and eclectic experimentation of the 1920s are also present in Rio Grande high style in the 1990s.

The Spanish Colonial Revival gained momentum in the 1920s

THE SPANISH COLONIAL REVIVAL OF NEW MEXICO

as wealthy patrons and commercial interests such as hotels, institutions, and artists became attracted to the fashionable movement. John Gaw Meem, an engineer who moved to Santa Fe in 1920 for health reasons, became an avid student of local architecture and thrived as he built houses for many distinguished clients in the years before the Depression.

Well-known artist and designer William Penhallow Henderson moved to Santa Fe from Boston in 1916. He also was swept up in the Revival fervor, building his studio in the foothills of Santa Fe in 1919, and featuring interior woodwork of his own design and craftsmanship.

New Mexico in the 1920s nurtured an entire generation of renaissance men and women, who were given an extraordinary opportunity to discover and reinterpret the ancient cultures of the Southwest. Among them, William Penhallow Henderson and Russian artist Nicolai Fechin in Taos created integrated architectural and furniture expressions in an ideosyncratic style but faithful to basic Spanish Colonial Revival and antimodernist ideals. Other students such as archaeologist Jesse Nusbaum and painter Carlos Vierra sought inspiration in New Mexico's long tradition of Spanish Colonial furniture and carving.

A concerted effort to preserve and promote the Spanish Colonial traditions of arts and crafts—furniture, textiles, tinwork, straw inlay, and other minor crafts—was organized by Frank Applegate, a ceramic artist and scholar who arrived in Santa Fe in 1921, and joined by writer Mary Austin. Applegate was well versed in the ideals of the English Arts and Crafts revival and envisioned a similar program in New Mexico.

Applegate's and Austin's efforts bore fruit in 1926 with the establishment of the Spanish Colonial Arts Society. The same year, the Society held its first exhibit during the Santa Fe Fiesta, and by 1928, the annual Spanish Market became firmly established.

After a period of spectacular growth and inspiration in the 1920s, the Spanish Colonial Revival faced more difficult conditions in the 1930s, primarily caused by the financial disaster of the Great Depression. The Spanish Colonial Arts Society opened a permanent store in Santa Fe for the marketing of local Hispanic arts and crafts in 1930, but the enterprise failed in 1933. In 1934, Leonora Curtin opened the Native Market, another sales outlet in Santa Fe, which lasted until 1940.

Unfortunately, poverty forced many village residents and artisans to seek employment in cities such as Albuquerque and Denver or as migrant farm workers. The pioneering work of Applegate, Austin, and the Spanish Colonial Arts Society enabled the State of New Mexico to create a unique vocational training program for Hispanic craftsmen after 1932.

With WPA and other federal work support funds, the Department of Vocational Education established schools in many Hispanic towns and villages throughout New Mexico to instruct and pay residents to learn traditional crafts. Most of the furniture and crafts produced under the auspices of the vocational schools was sold at the Native Market store in Santa Fe.

More importantly, under the direction of Bill Lumpkins, carefully measured drawings of nearly forty authentic examples of Spanish Colonial furniture were produced and bound in a shop manual for instructional use by the apprentices. The *Spanish Colonial Furniture Bulletins* of the New Mexico Department of Vocational Education, produced from 1933 to 1939, became the shop bibles for an entire generation of Hispanic furniture makers. Other publications in the series included *Spanish Colonial Painted Chests* (1937), *Graphic Standards for Furniture Designers* (1939), and *New Adaptations from Authentic Examples of Spanish Colonial Furniture* (n.d.).

Recently, William Wroth edited the finest of the measured drawings and produced a popular design book titled *Furniture from the Hispanic Southwest* (Ancient City Press, Santa Fe, 1984), and the legacy of the Spanish Colonial

Revival and the New Mexico Vocational Education Program thusly continues to influence contemporary, Rio Grande furniture makers.

The great experiment of vocational education in New Mexico during the 1930s, which trained a generation of craftsmen in traditional cabinetmaking, was to pay dividends for the United States

WORLD WAR II AND MODERNISM

war effort just a few years later. As the war approached in 1939, training emphasis switched to welding and sheet-metal work instead of cabinetmaking.

The war effort consumed the Spanish Colonial Revival as thousands

An armchair produced for the National Park Service's Regional Building in Santa Fe displays more generous proportions and heavier structural framing than Spanish Colonial prototypes. The Baroque and Pueblo Deco-inspired, carved details were typical of Spanish Colonial Revival furniture.

Master craftsman Elidio Gonzales of Taos, photographed here in the 1950s with his wife Guadalupe, perfected the Spanish Colonial Revival style. Gonzales, who died in 1988, influenced numerous contemporaries and apprentices, several of whom are still producing Spanish-style furniture of the Rio Grande.

of young men from New Mexico migrated to industrial jobs, mostly on the West Coast. World War II had other profound effects on New Mexican society. Perhaps the most profound of these was the adoption by many Hispanic-American veterans of the American Dream, a notion they had largely been shielded from in their isolation in rural New Mexico.

Many of these men and women encountered greater American society for the first time during the war years, discovering its advantages and prejudices. They learned English and suppressed their own native Spanish language; they realized the need for a higher education to succeed in the mainstream; and largely they yearned for the postwar normalcy of family life and the comforts of home that modern American technology provided. Manu-factured furniture and modern appliances, available through catalog retailers such as Montgomery Ward and Sears Roebuck, largely replaced handcrafted furniture in many New Mexican homes.

After the war, the first strides toward urbanism in New Mexico were made in Albuquerque, as the rapid growth of major institutions such as the University of New Mexico and cold-war employers such as Sandia National Laboratories and Kirtland Air Force Base further attracted village residents to city life. Higher paying machine and industrial jobs, the pursuit of higher education, and the raising of families discouraged the overwhelming majority of the Spanish Colonial Revival carpinteros from returning to their trade.

Although there remained a reasonable demand for Spanish Colonial furniture in New Mexico after the war, it was primarily desired by institutions such as universities and city halls and also by affluent Anglo-American

businesses and patrons. For the most part, New Mexican Spanish Colonial furniture made a transition from hand-craftsmanship before the war to machine tooling after the war, a change lamented by Roland Dickey in 1949 in his book *New Mexico Village Arts.*

"No longer sponsored by federal funds, the greater number of the native craftsmen who produced these pieces have turned to other work, but a few have continued to make a living at the age-old trades. The designs, especially in furniture, have been taken over by commercial shops, which employ power tools in producing the pieces demanded by modern offices, hotels, and restaurants, often merely adding ornament to factory items. . . .

As a result, not only is the piece shorn of individuality, rugged texture and intrinsic color, it has lost the indigenous qualities of struggle and spontaneity with which the old-time craftsman, by necessity, endowed it," (P. 244).

A few carpinteros continued the tradition of Spanish Colonial, hand-crafted furniture in the decades after World War II. Prominent among them were Abad Eloy Lucero of Albuquerque, Elidio Gonzales and Maximo Luna of Taos (both deceased), and George Sandoval of Albuquerque. All of these artists remained loyal to Spanish Colonial prototypes developed during the 1930s, retaining the generous proportions by which the Craftsman style influenced the Spanish Colonial pieces, especially in cabinets. Elidio Gonzales of Taos ran a successful furniture company, El Artesano de Taos, from 1945 until his death in 1988, developing a richly carved style. Elidio's work also exhibited a tendency towards Spanish provincial examples, often featuring complementary uphol-stery in leather or fine velvet.

Gonzales's longtime friend and teacher, Abad Lucero, still meticulously crafts Spanish Colonial furniture in his studio in Albuquerque. Lucero's work captures the refined essence of the Colonial aesthetic, maintaining ancient design motifs such as Maltese crosses and pine mortise-and-tenon joinery. Maximo Luna's work from Taos, where he practiced until his death in 1964, also shows a love of traditional Spanish designs. None of the postwar carpin-teros (with perhaps the exception of George Sandoval) exhibited a tendency to experiment with any painted finishes.

Only a few masters of the WPA and World War II generation perpetuated the tradition of Spanish Colonial furniture during the fifties and sixties in New Mexico. Mean-while, popular American taste in archi-tecture and furniture was making a transition from the sleek materials and refined elegance of the modernist aesthetic—the so-called Bauhaus and International styles—to a more person-ally crafted look.

POSTMODERNISM AND RIO GRANDE HIGH STYLE

Furniture style in the 1960s re-flected the topsy-turvy and controversial decade. American furniture design was breaking away from the cool sophis-tication of bent plywood, polished steel, and black leather, which characterized the best designs of modernist masters such as Charles Eames, Mies van der Rohe, and Eero Saarinen. After a flirtation with pop-art style such as beanbag chairs, furn-iture returned to a craftsman approach in the 1970s.

On the West Coast, architect Charles Moore signaled a reinvention of California vernacular architecture with his Sea Ranch of 1966. At the same time, on the west bank of the Rio Grande in Albuquerque, architect Antoine Predock began to redefine the Southwestern adobe vernacular with the La Luz Townhouses of 1966–1967.

Master furniture-maker Sam Maloof of California articulated a personal Craftsman style in the 1970s, combin-ing unparalleled craftsmanship with carefully selected fine and exotic woods. Maloof's example has inspired the Contemporary Craftsman style of furniture making, which still inspires several Rio Grande high-style masters.

In New Mexico by the mid-1970s, a new generation of young Hispanic *santeros,* furniture makers and woodcarvers of santos, had begun to produce remarkable work. Led by master craftsman Luis Tapia, who also carves impressive santos, newer artists began to be attracted once again to the Rio Grande furniture style after 1975.

This renewal of interest in traditional furniture and craftsmanship in the Southwest coincided with the rise of postmodernism in contemporary American architecture and design. Architectural historian Charles Jencks recalls in his book *The Language of Post-Modern Architecture* that

> *Newsweek* used the term "postmodern" ("Rise of the Come-Hither Look," January 17, 1977) to refer to the new, faceted, glass towers in America with their sleek, sensuous surfaces—otherwise not distinguishable from modern ones. Paul Goldberger (architecture critic of the *New York Times*) in articles on Charles Moore, Hardy, Holzman, Pfeiffer, and others has used it to refer to an architecture which is rich in symbolism and historical allusion (P. 8).

Still, postmodernism would not arrive in New Mexico as a viable design movement until the 1980s. After Santa Fe was rediscovered by the media, Hollywood, and upscale tourists by 1985, Rio Grande furniture was ready for its most current rebirth.

The postmodern sensibility as it relates to Rio Grande furniture encompasses more than the symbolism and historical allusion referred to by Paul Goldberger. Postmodernism also describes the sudden variety of construction and finishing techniques, materials, and seamless blending of styles and culturally based design motifs that now characterize the best of Rio Grande high style.

The dramatic canonization of Southwest or Santa Fe style as a chic new fashion by magazines such as *Metropolitan Home* and *House and Garden* and by architectural, interior, and fashion designers after 1985 has forever transformed Rio Grande high style. Only ten years ago, the familiar Spanish Colonial design still maintained its dominance in the marketplace. Today, at the close of the twentieth century, Rio Grande high style furniture has finally transcended its Spanish origins to become a truly original American style with substantial appeal in the national and international marketplace.

The metamorphosis from a regionally based furniture style to a national expression was created through innovations realized by New Mexico designers, combined with a fresh perspective and approach provided by talented designers from across the country.

During the five-year period from 1985 to 1990, two books played a pivotal role in the revival of interest in New Mexican furniture: *Santa Fe Style* by Christine Mather and *New Mexico Furniture 1600–1940* by Lonn Taylor and Dessa Bokides. In April 1988, *New Mexico* magazine joined numerous other publications with a cover story on New Mexico's hot furniture market.

The most significant innovation in New Mexican furniture in the post-World War II era has been the wild popularity of folk art-painted furniture, which arose in Taos in the 1980s. Led

La Placita
Old Albuquerque.
195

by Jim Wagner, a well-known Taos artist, the folk art furniture movement began modestly after 1980 in the scenic mountain home of the Taos Masters. Within a few years, the charming furniture, which borrowed basic Spanish Colonial forms and joinery but boasted lively, painted designs, had been discovered by major retailers such as Bloomingdale's and exclusive furnishing boutiques in Malibu, Los Angeles, San Francisco, Washington, D.C., and New York City.

The faddish popularity of Southwestern style after 1985 attracted other design influences, primarily from Los Angeles and New York, as Melrose Avenue and Soho retailers sought to cash in on the bonanza. Among the most popular of the new finishing techniques was "distressing," or the manipulation of the wood surface to achieve the illusion of age. Trasteros were beaten with chains, sandblasted, scratched, whitewashed, paint-stripped, along with other manipulations to simulate the real Spanish Colonial patina.

It was not long before Native American imagery was incorporated into Southwestern furniture. Petroglyph symbols, Navajo blanket designs, symbolic motifs such as clouds and sun, kachinas (images of the Pueblo gods), and Mimbres pottery designs have all found their way into postmodern Rio Grande furniture.

The use of a whole new palette of materials for furniture was another innovation of the 1980s. Classic western accessories such as bones, antlers, and bear claws were fashioned to adorn cabinets as pediment pieces or hardware such as door knobs and drawer pulls. A variety of leathers such as buckskin (rough and fringed), natural cow and deer hides, and fine Italian suede now contribute to the Rio Grande fashion.

Tinwork, a classic Spanish Colonial craft, has also been revived recently. Though tin panels (in trasteros and pie safes) and some tinwork details were made when the U.S. Army brought tin cans to New Mexico after 1850, tinwork largely disappeared from twentieth-century New Mexican furniture. Today,

The 1940s interior of Albuquerque's La Placita restaurant on the Old Town Plaza shows a simple and effective Rio Grande style. The seating is provided by Mexican equipale pigskin chairs, a design classic that is still popular in the Southwest.

both tinwork and copper are being exploited for their substantial decorative potential.

Textiles are yet another major area of discovery for Rio Grande design. Initially influenced by West Coast designers who imported Guatemalan and Oaxacan textiles, Rio Grande upholstered furniture and accessories such as throw pillows can acquire a Latin American or ethnic flavor. Southwestern sofas may be covered with Moroccan *kilims* (rugs or coverings), Pendleton blankets, or Chimayo weavings.

Stylistically, the Santa Fe-design boom also revived past Southwestern furniture traditions such as Mission/ Craftsman, Cowboy and Ranch, as well as architectural influences such as Pueblo Deco. As a result, within a ten-year period of phenomenal growth and metamorphosis, Rio Grande high style was created in the Southwestern United States, making an unprecedented quantum leap in which several historical styles have been revived simultaneously and a whole spectrum of materials and finishes have been introduced. As Rio Grande high style opened the 1990s, its influence was felt in nearly all parts of the United States as well as major design capitals nationally and internationally.

Rather than remaining exclusively loyal to successful products, leading Rio Grande designers have continued to develop exciting new expressions and product lines. The newest trends in Rio Grande high style include a redefinition of the Spanish Colonial aesthetic, the glamorization of the Mission/ Craftsman style, new development of Native American designs, fusion of traditional styles with ethnic, Third World motifs, and some inspiration from historical styles such as Art Deco and Classical.

The roots of Spanish Colonial style is becoming a popular new design opportunity for some craftsmen. Painted color and new hardwoods are also recharging the Rio Grande Spanish style.

Mission/Craftsman furniture is breaking free of its conservative dark oak and leather image. Lighter woods and aerodynamic-design profiles produce a surprisingly contemporary look.

In the 1990s, the American furniture industry is seeking new avenues of expression to serve a new clientele of consumers—the so-called MTV or X generation of people in their twenties or early thirties. Meanwhile, older homemakers, the post-World War II baby-boom generation, are remaining loyal to traditional styles such as Mission or Shaker or Spanish Colonial, seeking stability from the onslaught of computers, electronics, and high technology.

While many major American furniture manufacturers have incorporated mainstream Southwestern lines in their current offerings, such as Mission or painted Country Folk pieces, others are returning to modernist-inspired, contemporary furnishings to lure a younger clientele. The new movement in Eurostyle contemporary furniture is gaining popularity in urban centers while, simultaneously, many people are relocating to the West and Rocky Mountain states from the East and West coasts.

Though the public's fleeting fascination and appreciation of western style may ebb and flow, Rio Grande style has endured and matured for centuries. In the 1990s, the emergence and flourishing of major new talents and remarkable artistic innovation are sure to contribute to the saga of western design and the essence of Rio Grande high style.

THE NEW SPANISH STYLE OF THE SOUTHWEST

Our knowledge of furniture making in New Mexico during the Spanish Colonial era (1600–1820) is mostly one of romantic conjecture. The craftsmen who painstakingly pegged their chairs and chests together have remained anonymous; only their masterpieces speak to us.

NEW SPANISH CRAFTSMEN OF THE RIO GRANDE

The prize-winning *trastero/ropero* by Ramón José López is a standout, even amid the splendid array of furnishings and art in the East gallery of the Daniels house. Designed for the safekeeping of religious articles, it consists of twelve painted panels.

A collection of Spanish Colonial chairs from Latin America displays the heavy baroque character of Spanish furniture that currently influences some contemporary Rio Grande craftsmen.

Today we are fortunate to be witnessing the unfolding of a dramatic renaissance in Spanish furniture art in Rio Grande country, literally the development of a new Spanish style in the Southwest. At its core, the new Spanish style is being expressed by Hispanic and Anglo craftsmen, who together are introducing a wider spectrum of stylistic influences to Rio Grande Spanish style. The many facets of Spanish style itself, including Moorish, European Baroque, Spanish Provincial, and the more elaborate Spanish Colonial style of Mexico and Latin America, are now being manipulated by Rio Grande artists along with their own heritage of the New Mexican Spanish Colonial style.

Greg Flores of Taos embodies the spirit of the new Spanish style in New Mexico. Greg has refined the New Mexican Spanish Colonial aesthetic down to its essence—perfect proportions and simple ornamentation—achieving a Zen-like quality of harmony and refined elegance in his furniture.

His design philosophy is also straightforward. "What I am searching for in my work is purity. I'm attracted to purity in form, line, color, and propor-

A stately armoire, produced in the 1950s by Southwest Spanish Craftsmen of Santa Fe is ornamented by Spanish coat-of-arm motifs and impressive central roundels.

ON PURE EXPRESSION . . ."What I am searching for in my work is purity. I'm attracted to purity in form, line, color, and proportion. It's not something I consciously measure, but my eye tells me when I've got it. Sometimes, I make things that are off balance, and (I) keep making slight adjustments until I reach an expression that's simple, pure, and harmonious."

GREG FLORES, TAOS CRAFTSMAN

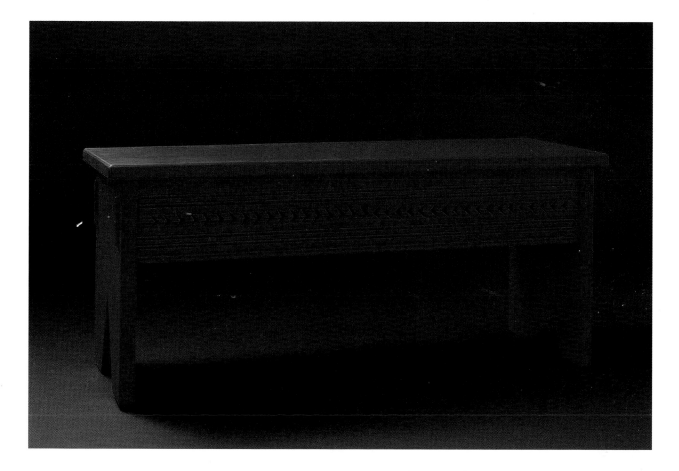

A humble, low bench becomes a remarkable exercise in rhythm in the hands of master craftsman Greg Flores of Taos.

tion. It's not something I consciously measure, but my eye tells me when I've got it. Sometimes I make things that are off balance and keep slightly making adjustments until I reach an expression that's simple, pure, and harmonious."

Greg Flores is a native of Taos and is largely a self-taught craftsman. While his furniture is classical and seemingly conservative, he also enjoys bold color, sometimes painting his cabinets blood red. The impulse to express bold color is fundamental to Hispanic art in the Americas, perhaps reflecting a subconscious tie to pre-Columbian and Native American sources.

Flores is one of a growing number of young master craftsmen who are elevating the centuries-old art form of Spanish furniture to a new plateau. The tradition and continued popularity of Rio Grande Spanish style is the heart and wellspring of all other Rio Grande styles. The names of these craftsmen will not be lost to history and memory. Many have already achieved a lasting reputation, and their furniture is being collected by museums and connoisseurs alike.

▲ traditional living-room ensemble by Taos Furniture includes seating
influenced by the deep lounges and settees of the Arts and Crafts movement.

A 1950s Santa Fe interior acquires a Spanish provincial personality with a massive baroque dining table and side chairs by Southwest Spanish Craftsmen. A wrought-iron wall chandelier and ceiling light fixture add to the Old World ambiance.

The baroque styling of Spanish provincial furniture is shown in a streamlined, round, iron-braced table and leather uphol-stered side chair by Southwest Spanish Craftsmen. The set was photographed in Santa Fe's Sena Plaza about 1960.

Spanish style along the Rio Grande has dramatically expanded its horizons recently, now expressing a wider range of the complex stylistic components of classic Hispanic furniture. Before making its appearance in the sixteenth-century New World, Hispanic furniture had been shaped and modified by several major Old World influences.

REVIVAL OF CLASSIC SPANISH STYLE

The long domination of Spain by the Moors from 711 to 1492 introduced a new level and style of crafts-manship that was combined with some European styling to create the distinctive Mudejar style. From the Moors, Spanish craftsmen and homemakers learned to appreciate the decorative arts of tooled leather, wrought iron, glazed and mosaic tile work, Oriental rugs and tapestries, and elaborately carved woodwork. These Moorish contributions to Spanish homestyle are still vital components of the Rio Grande high style.

Moorish carpenters developed a love of fancy-shaped and turned spindles, rich carving, and inlaid materials such as ivory and precious metal. Elaborate parquet designs in geometric or floral patterns signified the work of a master craftsman. Spanish designs combined these woodworking techniques with more traditional European forms such as chests, chairs, and tables to create distinctive Mudejar examples. Influences such as Italian Renaissance, French Gothic, and other Christian design motifs were common in Spanish furniture during the golden age of discovery (1492–1588).

A visit to the house and studio of the great Spanish artist El Greco (1541–1614) in Toledo, the ancient capital of Castile, reveals a glimpse of Spanish interior design during an era immediately preceding the colonization of New Mexico. This decor can thus be described as the root influence of contemporary Rio Grande style.

Turned, spindle-back chairs and storage chests carved in Mudejar style are displayed throughout the house. Tables with wrought-iron cross braces are a distinctive Spanish invention, but

apparently few were crafted in the Southwest during the Colonial period. Another familiar chair, the silla francesa (literally, a French-style chair) became known in New Mexico as a priest's chair, boasts throne-like proportions and stature, and is meant for the master of the house or a distinguished guest. A folding hip-joint chair of Italian origin never appeared in New Mexico.

Perhaps the most distinctive piece of Hispanic furniture, the vargueño (secretary) is common in El Greco's home. Design elements of the vargueño were incorporated into some New Mexican trasteros (the small drawers to store valuables, for example) during the colonial period, but a true vargueño crafted in New Mexico during the colonial period is rare or unknown. A few contemporary Rio Grande designers are making classic vargueños and other Mudejar-inspired furniture, as classic Spanish style is now being combined with the colonial examples to create a lively, new, creative interchange.

A New Mexican chest from the Spanish Colonial Era is painted in the exuberant decorative style influenced by Mexican furniture from the province of Michoacan.

The famous "Men in a Boat" painted chest by Southwest Spanish Craftsmen is a reproduction of the original in the Museum of New Mexico collection. The original chest was believed to have been made in the Chimayo region.

The carving on the front panel of a chest by Raymond Lopez of Santa Fe is a flawless formal design, incorporating a central rosette flanked by rampant lions and pomegranate plants.

In the modern era, from the Spanish Colonial Revival of the 1920s to the present, the technological innovation of power tools has generally enabled craftsmen to achieve more polished and refined furniture. Proportions have been increased to meet modern needs, and joinery is precise.

Decoratively, contemporary Spanish furniture of the Rio Grande features more elaborate carving than the colonial prototypes. Today's Spanish furniture of the Southwest can thus range from baroque-carving effects more familiar in Spain or Latin America, to intricate Moorish geometric designs, to simple cutout shapes of the colonial period.

Perhaps the most distinctive innovation in Spanish style is the broad range of painted finishes now available. Colonial furniture was painted on occasion, though painted designs were generally reserved for chests and trasteros. A few rare examples of

pictorial images exist, such as the famous "men in a boat" chest reproduced by Southwest Spanish Craftsmen, but designs usually followed basic symbolic (hearts and crosses) or floral imagery.

The availability of paint imported from the eastern United States via the Santa Fe Trail, and later the railroad, radically transformed New Mexican furniture design. Entire cabinets, chairs, and tables were painted, often in charming folk designs or naive interpretations of Victorian styles popular in the decades preceding the turn of the century. This late nineteenth-century, Sangre de Cristo Country folk style is still a powerful influence on Rio Grande Design, inspiring both the Spanish and Taos Country artists.

Twentieth-century Spanish furniture of the Rio Grande was redefined by master designers of the Revival period such as Jesse Nusbaum and William Penhallow Henderson. Besides carving in a personal style, these artists also introduced Arts and Crafts and Art Deco

Federico Prudencio of Albuquerque apprenticed with Elidio Gonzales of Taos, continuing the tradition of baroque Spanish Colonial furniture, which became popular in New Mexico after the Great Depression.

ON INSPIRATION . . . *"New Mexico is so visual; there's a lot of interesting colors and textures all around. . .I'll get ideas for new pieces just driving between Albuquerque and Santa Fe and looking at the landscape. . .*

"I also study the old (furniture) pieces and look for details that I like. . .We have so many influences to choose from here. For our Sandia (lounge) chair, I just really liked the curve of a chair arm that was made in New Mexico in the nineteenth century that has a classical, Empire-style profile. So I just refined it a little bit and expanded the proportions to modern dimensions. It's been a great seller for us."

MIKE GODWIN, ERNEST THOMPSON FURNITURE

Ernest Thompson Furniture of Albuquerque is among the most progressive and innovative of all Rio Grande furniture companies. The Tesuque Dining Collection capitalizes on a fundamental Spanish Colonial-design motif, the carved rope, and repeats it effectively on the dining table, side chairs, and buffet.

▲
Ernest Thompson Furniture's "Chief" dining-room set reveals finely carved and painted Pueblo Deco styling, which modifies traditional Pueblo Indian designs in a modern and geometric way.
▼

ON INSPIRATION . . . *"One thing that I really appreciate is the fact that New Mexico has a long tradition of furniture makers. Some places are richer in cabinetmakers. But here, the craftsmen are trained to think in three dimensions, and the furniture has a wonderful, sculptural quality."*

DOREEN GODWIN, ERNEST THOMPSON FURNITURE

Artworks in the chapel of Lopez' Santa Fe house are full of meaning. The bed was the Grand Prize winner of the 1993 Traditional Spanish Market. The six panel altar screen—Lopez' gift to his wife Nance—won the Grand Prize in 1989.

Ramon Jose Lopez has maintained a preeminent status among New Mexico santeros, the artists who create religious figures. Devoted to the expression of Spanish Colonial art, Lopez has also made a few distinctive furniture pieces of the highest caliber, painting them in a refined, classic style.

Lopez grew up and now lives in Santa Fe. He is a regular prizewinner at the annual Spanish Market held each July. Recently, a Spanish Colonial bed he fashioned won a top prize. Together with his santos and the timeless adobe architecture of the region, Lopez's furniture creates an aesthetically pure expression, something akin to devotion and reverence.

sensibilities in some of their pieces.

After World War II, Spanish furniture design in New Mexico reverted to a colonial and conservative approach perpetuated by a few masters such as Elidio Gonzales of Taos and Abad Lucero and George Sandoval of Albuquerque. Their legacy was inherited by younger craftsmen such as Luis Tapia and Greg Flores in the 1970s and 1980s.

The current and recent atmosphere of revival and flourishing of the Rio Grande style has elevated furniture making in many cases above mere utilitarian purpose. Hispanic furniture has become not only a vehicle for artistic expression by artists, craftsmen, and designers, it has also become a collectible art form, prized by the marketplace.

This phenomenon has encouraged a crossover of design talent in Spanish style, notably fostering a creative interchange between the religious art of the santeros and the furniture craft of the carpinteros. As a result, established Hispanic artists such as Luis Tapia and Ramon Jose Lopez are crafting furniture but decorating their work in a manner derived from the process and style of Colonial religious art. The santero-inspired furniture is an emerging design motif in contemporary Spanish style of the Rio Grande.

Other young masters, notably Chris Sandoval and Greg Flores, are forging a contemporary personal aesthetic inspired by traditional Colonial design motifs but tempered by the streamlined appeal of modernism. Sandoval's palette of color finishes and incorporation of some Native American imagery gives his work a sophisticated, New Age appeal firmly rooted in the New Mexican tradition. Greg Flores has evolved a sublime and elegant style characterized by clean precision, perfect proportions, minimal ornamentation, and sometimes bold color.

▲ The Truchas rope-carved, four-poster bed is Ernest Thompson's variation on a Rio Grande Spanish-style favorite. ▼

Several furniture companies have played a vital role in perpetuating and popularizing the Spanish tradition in New Mexico. Southwest Spanish Craftsmen, Taos Furniture, and Ernest Thompson Furniture have maintained long traditions of stylistic integrity and excellence. Newer companies contributing to Spanish style include Dell Woodworks, Doolings of Santa Fe, and Blue Canyon Woodworks.

Breaking free of the Colonial tradition and yet continuing to celebrate and articulate it is the current attitude of Spanish designers. In this regard, the recent decade from 1985 to 1995 represents the liveliest burst of creativity since the 1920s or the 1880s. The design world is currently enjoying a major revival and renaissance of Spanish style in the greater Southwest.

▲

Taos Furniture of Santa Fe has been producing exceptional Spanish Colonial furniture faithful to the New Mexican tradition since before 1970. Taos Furniture's extensive line features many authentic reproductions of historic Spanish Colonial examples, including this Taos Governor's trastero reproduced in Alan Vedder's book *Furniture of Spanish New Mexico*.

▼

PAUL MARTINEZ
TAOS, NEW MEXICO

Paul Martinez prides himself as a Taos woodworker, claiming to be inspired by the town's master, Elidio Gonzalez, who died about a decade ago. Paul's furniture maintains the massive elegance of the Spanish Colonial style, as practiced in the traditional way.

Still, Taos works its magic on all artists, and Paul's furniture boasts distinctive flourishes, such as carved scenes of Taos Pueblo on door panels. What distinguishes Paul Martinez's work is the magnificent carving—precise but proudly displaying the marks of chisel and caress of hand. Martinez's work is naturally finished and has won numerous awards, including a first-prize ribbon at the annual Spanish Market in Santa Fe.

A remarkable door by Paul Martinez of Taos features a carved representation of Taos Pueblo on its central panel.

Luis Tapia

Contemporary artist Luis Tapia of Santa Fe has invented a personal visual expression of New Mexican religious art and furniture. Working with a strong palette reflecting a modern taste rather than traditional, Tapia has created a *trompe l'oeil* trastero. This trastero could be described as a fascinating example of postmodernism or the santero style in Rio Grande Spanish style.

An impressive trastero by Michael Trujillo of Taos makes effective use of turquoise paint detailing to give the design an unmistakable Rio Grande heritage.

The opposed-diamonds design featured on Taos Furniture's priest bedframe and armoire is a classic motif that the company has made famous.

Gunther Worrlein's contemporary Spanish bench, commissioned for the New Mexico State Capitol, is a masterpiece of Rio Grande high style. A pleasing rhythm is created by the repeated row of rampant lions framed by a scalloped border, which is repeated in the front bench skirt below.

GEORGE AND CHRIS SANDOVAL
ALBUQUERQUE, NEW MEXICO

George Sandoval and his son Chris exemplify the true spirit of master and apprentice. George is one of the senior Hispanic furniture makers in New Mexico and has been crafting superb Spanish Colonial furniture in his studio in Albuquerque for over forty years.

As a boy, Chris used to sweep up the wood shavings in his father's studio, and the love of working with wood was naturally ingrained in him. Recently, Chris formed a new furniture company with partner, Mark Carrico, called Artisans of the Desert. As a contemporary Rio Grande furniture maker, Chris loves the geometric interplay of the Art Deco style and tries to fuse it with traditional Spanish Colonial forms.

A contemporary Rio Grande armchair by Chris Sandoval of Albuquerque is influenced by Art Deco styling.

Greg Flores

Maltese crosses, handcrafted latch and door hinges, and brilliant red color combine to superb effect in a nightstand by Taos craftsman Greg Flores.

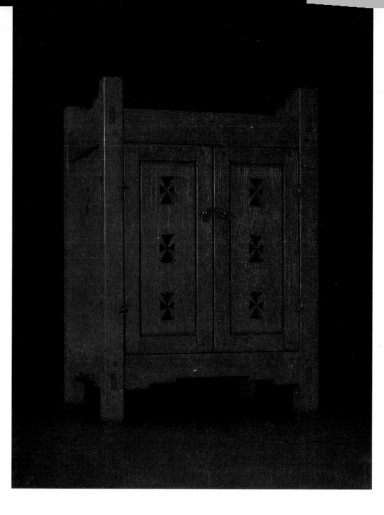

Blue Canyon

The opposing rails and slats of Blue Canyon Woodworks' "Galisteo" bench, a reproduction of a nineteenth-century original, illustrates the New Mexican technique of creating a pleasing design with multiple repeating slats or flat spindle shapes.

SOUTHWEST SPANISH CRAFTSMEN
SANTA FE, NEW MEXICO

Among the Southwest's premier furniture studios, Southwest Spanish Craftsmen of Santa Fe also has the distinction of being the oldest. This remarkable company has produced high quality Spanish furniture since the late 1920s.

Although the studio has a reputation for producing furniture that boasts a rich and traditional Old World appeal, the designs are by no means static. Among its current offerings are tables carved and painted with Pueblo designs, and easy chairs and sofas displaying Arts and Crafts-style influences.

Southwest Spanish Craftsmen's distinctive offerings are primarily Spanish Provincial, a European style, and the unmistakable Spanish Colonial style of New Mexico. The Spanish Provincial collection features massive tables richly carved with baroque designs, elegant Spanish chairs with smooth leather seats, and classic highboy cabinets.

Besides reproducing museum-quality pieces such as eighteenth-century painted chests and carved trasteros, Southwest Spanish Craftsmen is also inventive in its Colonial line, incorporating beautifully crafted tin panels on bed headboards and chests.

Over the years, Southwest Spanish Craftsmen has proven its ability to maintain a fine balance between the classic, traditional look and the innovative, trendy cycles of design. Its palette of materials, finishes, and repertoire has evolved and been refined over many years and is a hallmark of excellence in Rio Grande design.

▲ **A** priest's chair by Southwest Spanish Craftsmen is faithful to original armchairs produced during the Spanish Colonial era. Only the clergy and very wealthy families on the New Mexican frontier were able to afford the expensive manufacture of the amply proportioned and ornamented chairs. ▼

▲ **S**outhwest Spanish Craftsmen's La Madera chest is a reproduction of a chest in the Taos style. Heavy, Moorish chip-carving characterized a series of remarkable furniture produced in the northern Rio Grande area about 1800. ▼

A living-room suite by Southwest Spanish Craftsmen of Santa Fe epitomizes contemporary Rio Grande Spanish style. In the foreground, the Antigua chair and ottoman reflect Arts and Crafts influence and New Mexican chip-carving technique. The Mimbres highboy is a European cabinet adorned with Native American pottery designs of the prehistoric Mimbres culture of southwestern New Mexico. The big Tesuque chair in the background combines Spanish Colonial and Provincial styles accented with a Navajo blanket-style upholstery.

ABAD LUCERO
ALBUQUERQUE, NEW MEXICO

Now in his mid-eighties, Abad Lucero is the senior master craftsman among New Mexico's Hispanic furniture makers. Lucero taught himself the art and craft of furniture making during the Great Depression, learning the fine points from measured drawings of classic furniture that he received from his friend, architect Bill Lumpkins.

Lucero also worked with Elidio Gonzales in Taos for a while before eventually moving to Albuquerque. Abad has now completed a lifetime of projects but keeps himself young by continuing to visit the shop every day and working on new projects.

Lucero's work is massive and classic, adorned by the ancient rosettes and Maltese crosses of Spain. He still takes pride in using very few nails in his work, relying on the integrity of true mortise-and-tenon joinery. For Abad Lucero, "Spanish Colonial furniture might not be elaborate in detail, but it must meet the requirements for durability and comfort."

▲ **A** detail of Abad Lucero's reproduction of a Spanish Colonial pie safe focuses on a handmade iron latch. ▼

▲ **A**bad Lucero designed this saddleback chair in the Spanish Provincial style in the 1930s. The chair is constructed of handmade nails and heavy leather. ▼

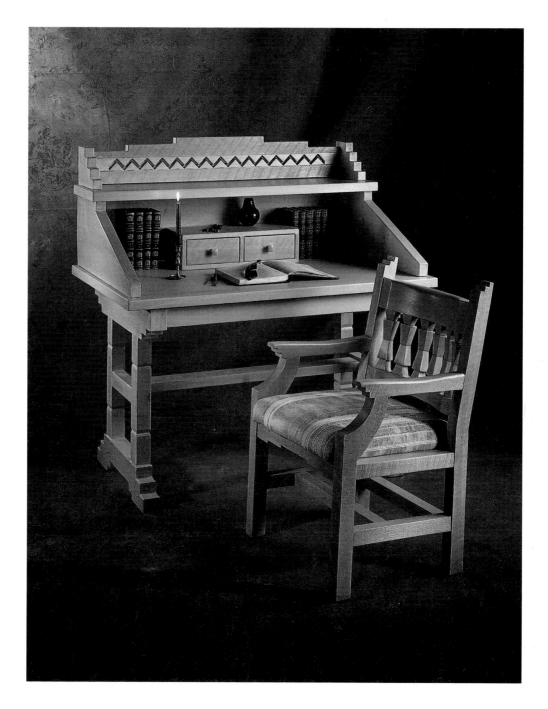

A handsome desk set by Dell Woodworks of Santa Fe combines classic Pueblo stepped and zigzag designs with fine traditional craftsmanship to produce an extraordinary Rio Grande ensemble.

TAOS
COUNTRY

Just north of Espanola Valley, past the small orchard villages of Embudo and Dixon, and through a magnificent gorge deeply cut by the churning waters of the Rio Grande, the town of

Taos looms regally beneath its crown of rugged mountains. Taos is a sacred name in the Rocky Mountains, the goal of a steady stream of adventurers and creative spirits for over 500 years.

The interior of Nicolai Fechin's house in Taos displays some of his signature, carved-furniture pieces and architectural elements. Dramatic architectural expressions, such as the fireplace and a sweeping curved wall at left, together with art and furniture give the Fechin house an intriguing Asian character.

A casual visitor to Taos will instantly sense something different and exotic—a free and lively splash of color here and there, a light-headed feeling of invigoration. The complex mixture of aesthetics and culture that has shaped Rio Grande high style is nowhere more apparent than on the streets of Taos.

The magnificent Taos Pueblo, founded about the fourteenth century, represents the epitome of post-Anasazi pueblo architecture. There, Taos residents hosted a scouting party of the Coronado expedition of 1540.

Various Spanish settlements struggled to gain a foothold beneath the Taos Mountains in the seventeenth century before the successful Pueblo Revolt of 1680 cut them short. Not until after 1750 were the Spanish able to sustain a community in the remarkably beautiful Taos Valley.

Taos served as a natural base for mountain men and trappers; its famous Taos Lightning whiskey and lively women were the source of countless legends and wild tales of the Old West. Later, Taos welcomed the wagon caravans of the Mountain Branch of the Santa Fe Trail (1821–1879), an era that witnessed the phenomenal rise of a wiry and fearless scout, Kit Carson.

In September 1898, artists Ernest Blumenschein and Bert G. Phillips wrecked their wagon on a dirt road near Taos, and their impression of being stranded in northern New Mexico turned from frustration to a sense of awe and fascination with the landscape. With these two remarkable men, the Taos Society of Artists was founded, and it flourished with the original members until World War II.

Taos was a well-kept secret until the 1920s, when it lured Mabel Dodge Stern, famed New York socialite, and her entourage, which eventually included D. H. Lawrence. Mabel later wrote, "Nobody had ever heard of New Mexico until I went there."

Nicolai Fechin

A threshhold inside the Nicolai Fechin house in Taos displays the inventiveness by which the artist fused Spanish Colonial and Russian folk art techniques.

▲
Nicolai Fechin's impressive genius for woodcarving is evident in a shelf unit and table he produced for his house in Taos during the years 1927 to 1933. These pieces are predominantly expressive of Russian folk art motifs.
▼

Taos still retains its lustre as one of the the world's celebrated art colonies, regularly attracting fine artists, writers, sculptors, and poets. Therefore, it is not surprising that this remarkable and sometimes eccentric town on the northern Rio Grande has spawned its own furniture style—Taos Country.

The bright and colorful furniture we identify today as Taos Country has its spiritual beginnings in the interiors of

EVOLUTION OF TAOS COUNTRY

several famous Taos citizens. In the parlor of the Kit Carson home, now a downtown museum, visitors detect a refined taste in Eastern furniture (in this case, Eastlake style), displayed in a traditional, New Mexican adobe interior, which is illustrative of the Yankee and New Mexican-hybrid style of the Santa Fe Trail days.

Ernest Blumenschein's living room displays antique examples of Spanish

Colonial furniture alongside Mexican pigskin, equipale chairs. Mabel Dodge Stern's four-poster bed is an interesting adaptation of classic Spanish salomonic columns (resembling twisted rope) to a furniture use.

The sense of artistic inventiveness that characterizes Taos Country furniture has its aesthetic roots in the home of Nicolai Fechin, a Russian artist who resided in Taos from 1927 to 1933. A master woodcarver, Fechin adapted Russian folk art designs to New Mexican furniture forms, such as the trastero and chest, and to architectural features such as columns and corbels. Fechin reproductions are available today from Jeremy Morrelli Studio of Santa Fe.

During the post-World War II years, Spanish Colonial masters Elidio Gonzales and Max Luna associated with the Vocational Education program of the 1930s, successfully carrying on the furniture tradition in Taos. Other Hispanic craftsmen, active in Taos before and during the rise of Taos Country style, included Antonio Archuleta, Mark Romero, Eduardo Lavadie, and Gilbert Vargas.

After 1981, longtime Taos artist Jim Wagner, whose paintings are characterized by a light yet bold palette, began to paint folk art furniture after being asked to decorate a pair of old doors by a friend. In 1981, Wagner and partners Tony Martinez and Tony

TAOS COUNTRY FURNITURE

Country Furnishings of Taos showrooms in Taos display a variety of design effects by employing Taos Country-style products. A variety of brightly painted folk art furniture is accented by ceramics and wrought-iron house furnishings. The Taos Country look, above all, is colorful and playful.

This distinctive cabinet by Jim Wagner celebrates a common sight in New Mexico, a flock of busy magpies.

Hillary Riggs

Hillary Riggs's son Alex Nugent helped inspire the design of the unique "27 Little Pigs" screen, a classic of the Taos Country aesthetic.

Lopez formed a business called Trasteros, Inc., and began selling their furniture as fast as they could make it. A two-door trastero in those days sold for only $100.

Although Trasteros, Inc., was short-lived, Wagner and Martinez persevered by establishing a unique cooperative with the Taos County Adult Probation office to train both adult and juvenile offenders in furniture making. Called Muebles de Taos, the program succeeded in popularizing the new Taos furniture style but ultimately failed for lack of capital support.

In 1986, a small retail store called Taos Country Furnishings, owned by Mary and Dana Shriver, agreed to carry Wagner's line. After Wagner's folk furniture was discovered by Bloomingdale's

shortly thereafter, a media blitz of articles by national publications such as the *New York Times,* the *Philadelphia Inquirer,* and *Glamour* magazine further escalated the status of Taos Country furniture and helped fuel the Santa Fe-design boom of the late 1980s. A 1988 cover article in *New Mexico* magazine, featuring a Wagner trastero on the cover, officially recognized Taos Country as an original, New Mexico furniture expression.

Since the heady breakthrough days of the early 1980s, Taos Country has spread its influence throughout the West and the entire furniture industry, contributing substantially to the popularity of American Country furniture in the 1980s. Sold by several exclusive interior designer boutiques

ON TECHNIQUE . . .

"A lot of furniture makers look for the best woods, the best grain. Not me. Whenever I'd get a piece of wood with a defect in it, I'd call attention to it, make something out of it. One time I got a board with a pretty bad split in it, and I filled it with mud and painted over it. Took it to the gallery and sold it right away.

"I married a woman from Talpa (a small village near Taos), and I was exposed to furniture in the village. Wonderful stuff! . . . People just had it in their homes and thought nothing of it. But I was fascinated by the naive quality of it. Just great! I remember seeing a bench in the Millicent Rogers Museum. It looked like the carpenter was trying to imitate a French Rococo style, and it wasn't quite right, but then it was! For me, naive art is the truest art in the world."

JIM WAGNER, TAOS ARTIST

▲
Jim Wagner
▼

An inlaid and painted, tile tabletop by Jim Wagner has the character of New Mexican retablo art, or the religious art painted on flat, lightly carved, wooden wall plaques by artists called santeros.

▲
The "Angel" trastero, a recent piece by Jim Wagner, plays delightfully with a New Age theme. The inset, punched-tin panel recalls classic New Mexican pie-safe trasteros.
▼

Peter Gould & Hillary Riggs

Towering August sunflowers are captured on carved, inset panels on a
magnificent trastero by Peter Gould and Hillary Riggs.

Poppies in full bloom are carved on a matching bed set by designers Hillary Riggs and Peter Gould.

on Hollywood's Melrose Avenue and other locations in southern California and San Francisco, Taos Country style became a favorite of movie stars, popular entertainers, and other urban trendsetters.

In New Mexico and other parts of the Southwest, Taos Country caused a sensation among artists and craftsmen, attracting many fine artists to experiment with furniture design. Today, Taos Country style is well established, achieving the status of instant Rio Grande high style and western furniture classic. Though Jim Wagner is not as active in furniture art as he was ten years ago, he still continues to make occasional pieces, which are exhibited at the Parks Gallery in Taos.

Robert Brenden

A nicho by Robert Brenden is whimsical and charming, an ode to watermelons. The frame itself is based on the classical, Greek Revival style that was blended with Spanish Colonial adobes by U.S. Army builders to create New Mexico's Territorial style.

THE DIXON TRADITION

About twenty or thirty miles downriver from Taos, near a narrow canyon where the Rio Grande is squeezed into a surging fury, the small Hispanic village of Dixon is nestled among picturesque orchards and farmland. After the cultural revolution of the 1960s, both Taos and Dixon (and other nearby villages) attracted creative people fleeing urban, industrial lifestyles.

Dixon is a small, tightly knit village of several hundred people that fostered an alternative artistic version of Taos Country style in the 1980s. Developed in a collaborative process by artists such as Michael Wildgoose and Hillary Riggs, Dixon furniture utilized slender, precisely cut, willow branches as inset panels and decorative accents on simply crafted cabinets.

In the past few years, the Dixon willow style has evolved aesthetically into an elegant, sophisticated appeal. The coloring of the willow branches by painting and dyeing techniques, combined with the painting of the furniture in contrasting or complementary schemes, produces a striking effect.

Artist Robert Brenden of Dixon has developed an alternative Taos Country expression, primarily based in the folk architecture of New Mexico's territorial period (1848–1912) when American and Victorian sensibilities transformed New Mexico's buildings and furniture. Greek Revival motifs, such as pediments and Victorian gingerbread cutout shapes, were adapted by Brenden who applies dazzling painted color to produce charming folk harmonies on trasteros, shelves, and nichos.

Robert Brenden is a native of Denver who has now settled in the picturesque village of Dixon, located about thirty miles south of Taos. Brenden is fascinated by the relationship between music, geometry, color, and ornament—influences that are readily apparent in his work.

In Brenden's summary, "While there are some who lament the demise of the International style, I myself do not. It seems that I have been postmodern for the past twenty-five years without knowing it. I've always enjoyed combining disparate elements and watching them coalesce in brightly colored, architecturally influenced constructions and shrines. There is always a feeling of surprise and delight that keeps me exploring new design possibilities. I call my style Territorial Baroque."

Brenden's work is inspired by the territorial architecture of northern New Mexico, a style introduced by the U.S. Army at forts in New Mexico after 1850, and is still popular in the state. It's a blend of Greek Revival elements and New Mexican architecture and carpentry. In northern New Mexico, the style was interpreted by isolated carpenters and furniture makers, creating a charming folk expression.

▲
A room in Robert Brenden's Dixon home displays a collection of baskets, bird cages, and a Territorial-style bench whose scrolled rails are based on turn-of-the-century prototypes.
▼

▲
Dixon artist Robert Brenden has developed a furniture style that he calls Territorial Baroque. The term refers to a style of carpentry that evolved in New Mexico after 1850, when Yankee tools and Victorian taste transformed the traditional Spanish Colonial aesthetic. A nicho (wall shelf) by Brenden exploits the folk art possibilities of this jigsaw style.
▼

Michael Wildgoose

Dixon craftsman Michael Wildgoose helped pioneer the popular, painted willow inlay that became a distinctive design element of the Santa Fe-furniture boom in the 1980s. A screen by Wildgoose has an elegant Southwest Deco design.

Michael Wildgoose's willow trastero boasts a handsome herringbone pattern similar to the technique used to construct ceilings in traditional Spanish Colonial adobe homes in New Mexico.

In the 1990s, Taos Country style continues to inspire new artists, who are producing exciting variations of a refined country style with an artistic

TAOS COUNTRY STYLE OF THE 1990S edge. Christopher Woolam paints his finely crafted furniture with realistic, sometimes humorous, images of the New Mexican landscape. The vast and dynamic Rio Grande sky is a major theme in his work along with pristine landscapes and the occasional beat-up pickup truck. Woolam's work is a natural progression in the Taos tradition, evocative of the fine art of the Taos Masters.

Teresa Swayne's furniture is faithful to mainstream country style in its basic forms but reflects the Taos taste in its occasional, brightly painted finishes and decorative flourishes. Mark Manville also crafts country furniture, incorporating meticulously crafted copper and steel panels and vibrant color.

True to its home source, Taos Country style is the product of brilliant individual creativity rather than a traditional, follow-the-rules approach. Such a movement is prone to the unpredictable cycles of creativity and repose, genius and mediocrity. Yet Taos has blessed Rio Grande high style and the furniture industry with a fresh new art form still aspiring to reach maturity. While its future expression is still developing, Taos Country style has already delighted and charmed many connoisseurs of fine furniture.

▲

Chris Woolam

▼

A masterful "Mountain Meadow" trastero by Chris Woolam displays extraordinary carving and painting effects. The piece has a Pueblo Deco character due to its stylized cloud and lightning designs.

Taos Country furniture has evolved in the 1990s to a remarkable expression combining carpentry, fine art, whimsy, and a bit of Spanish Colonial tradition. All of these elements are present in the furniture art of Christopher Woolam.

Woolam was trained as an engineer, served in the Peace Corps, and finally discovered his muse as a builder and furniture maker after settling in northern New Mexico with his wife Marion and their two children.

Woolam's furniture employs traditional, Spanish Colonial mortise-and-tenon joinery and popular forms such as benches and trasteros. He has created his own signature-carved flourishes, including animals and plants (corn, chilies, fish, toucans).

The meticulously painted scenes of ordinary life in northern New Mexico are extraordinary in their pictorial realism. Explaining his art, Woolam observes, "The idea of painted furniture is not new, being popular in Europe and as far back as ancient Egypt. However, it is usually a collaboration between artist and artisan. Since I do all the woodworking, carving, and painting, I feel that my pieces are unique.

"My inspiration comes from many sources . . . the magical and mystical beauty of the Southwestern landscape, my observations of plants and animals and experiences as a Peace Corps volunteer in South America and as a traveler in other parts of the world. Using furniture itself as a canvas, I design and then construct a useful piece that I feel best expresses a particular theme."

▲ A Parsons table by artist Christopher Woolam of Taos is a blend of Spanish Colonial style and Taos Country artistry. The central rosette and spiral column legs are ancient Spanish forms, and the New Mexico landscape is meticulously painted.
▼

Beat-up pickup trucks still working in the mountains of New Mexico are an enduring image for contemporary artists. Chris Woolam's "Red Pickup" bench captures the charming scene, complete with carved coyotes running across the crest of the piece.

Mary Shriver, with a lump in her throat and a tear in her eye, recalls the first heady days of the birth of Taos Country furniture. "Almost all of us in Taos owe something to Jim Wagner. . . . I started working in Jim's studio in the fall of 1986. Jim had this pet piglet called Truffles, and part of my job was to look after it. So I was taking care of Truffles and sanding furniture at the same time. Well, you know how big and fast pigs grow! . . . pretty soon, watching Truffles was almost a full-time job!"

After Jim Wagner's furniture business skyrocketed, he persuaded Mary to open a retail outlet. "Jim didn't want to be in the mass-production business. He felt that his pieces were one-of-a-kind collectibles. . . . So there I was, not knowing anything about business, but I plunged into it. I found a great house in Taos (for my gallery) that used to be the obstetrician's office, and local people still come by to peek at the room where they were born. . . . Taos-style furniture sold itself back then. People ask me how I did my marketing; basically, I just had to open the door each morning, and the business walked in."

Today, Mary's company, Taos Country Furniture, still thrives, producing the charming folk furniture that is the bedrock of Taos Country style. Local craftsmen Pedro Chavez, Jerome Montoya, Kelvin Sandoval, Richard Nelson, Eugene Ramsey, Anita McDaniel, Jamison Welles, Christine Waszak, and Cynthia Roberts build and paint the furniture.

The secret of Taos Country Furn-iture's appeal is its fresh and innovative dynamic. "I let the craftsmen come up with the designs. . . . They deserve all the credit. So we always have a 'new' look and new products to offer," Mary says.

Theresa Swayne

Trasteros by Theresa Swayne of Taos feature an exciting juxtaposition of paint, cabinet design, and metal inlaid panels. Swayne's style is precise; proportions and designs are carefully measured and executed, but the overall effect is an original expression of Taos Country style.

MISSION FURNITURE OF THE SOUTHWEST

Santa Fe craftsman Randolph Laub went against the grain as a young boy while growing up in Southern California. At the height of the cultural revolution of the 1960s, when many of his contemporaries were installing black lights and collecting pop furniture such as beanbag chairs, Randolph was collecting cast-off, heavy, oak furniture in the Arts and Crafts style by Gustav Stickley.

Berkeley Mills Studio

Originally based in Berkeley, California, Berkeley Mills Studio established a branch office in Santa Fe a few years ago. Berkeley Mills' distinctive style of Mission furniture is influenced by Japanese styling and exotic woods.

Though often referred to as the Pueblo Revival style, New Mexico's Mission Revival style was created in large part by the surprising synthesis of Spanish Colonial mission facades expressed in the New Mexico building at the 1915 Panama-California Exposition in San Diego, California.

Laub has been immersed in the Craftsman tradition and philosophy for most of his life, gaining firsthand exposure to the architecture of Greene and Greene and entire neighborhoods of early twentieth-century bungalows in the Los Angeles area. Later, he studied design at the Art Center of Los Angeles.

As with most champions of the Arts and Crafts tradition, for Laub the Craftsman philosophy, style, and way of life are one and the same. In contrast to furniture full of "contraption and silly gargoyles," Laub seeks an expression of nobility, simplicity, and integrity. In a refined furniture style with few apparent construction and ornamental details, they must be perfectly executed. There is very little room for error or imprecision.

Such high standards have made Randolph Laub one of the nation's foremost Arts and Crafts furniture makers. After moving to Santa Fe over ten years ago, Laub opened a studio and began producing distinctive Craftsman furni-

ture and also exceptional, fine art picture frames. His reputation and business grew steadily; at one point he employed thirteen craftsmen.

Laub decided to drastically reduce his work force when he realized that his studio was producing and shipping furniture he hadn't inspected. Today, Randolph has returned to the artist-as-craftsman practice, which is at the heart of his aesthetic and ethic. Each piece of Laub furniture is an original, caressed by the master himself.

A Morris chair by Randolph Laub of Santa Fe offers lighter, more streamlined proportions than the original Craftsmen prototypes.

In contrast to the glitzy "Wall Street" 1980s, the 1990s are charac-

RISE OF THE MISSION REVIVAL STYLE

terized by sober "Main Street" practicality. Bold, colorful Southwestern style, epitomized by whimsical, painted Taos trasteros, took the design world by storm nearly ten years ago; but now, aging baby boomers are seeking more conservative home furnishings.

Forsaken and scorned by hip modernists after 1930, the simple, durable craftsmanship and natural finishes of Mission style or Arts and Crafts furniture are now once again in demand.

Neo-Mission-style arcades, verandas, courtyards, and mission church facades are providing new design inspiration for architects and builders across the Spanish Southwest, from California to New Mexico and beyond to Florida.

While Victorian architectural styles such as Italianate and Queen Anne were still popular in New Mexico towns in 1885, the seeds of a new design sensibility were already being sown in California, the eastern United States, and England. The promoters of the Arts and Crafts movement preached a way of life based on pure, natural design,

Sylvanus G. Morley enjoyed a distinguished career as an eminent Mayan scholar and helped lead the Pueblo Revival movement in Santa Fe in the early twentieth century. A view of Morley's Santa Fe living room in 1912 shows an appreciation of the Mission style in furniture and interior design.

The interior of the New Mexico building at the Panama-California Exposition featured heavy-beamed ceilings and white stucco walls evocative of the original Rio Grande Mission style.

honest craftsmanship, organic colors, and quality materials.

The surging popularity of the Arts and Crafts movement after 1885 coincided perfectly with the rediscovery of Southwestern Mission architecture. Californian Helen Hunt Jackson's fabulously popular book *Ramona*, published in 1884, painted a sentimental, ambrosian picture of life and romance in the California mission, and together with Charles Lummis's exhortations, the foundation was prepared for the Mission Revival style.

To an emerging American nation,

healing from the wounds of the Civil War, tired of Victorian exuberance and excess ornament, and fascinated with the western frontier, the appeal of a new architecture based on southwestern mission church forms was spontaneous. The Mission Revival style was quickly espoused by the Atchison, Topeka, and Santa Fe Railroad as its official style in the 1890s.

Santa Fe hospitality wizard Fred Harvey created romantic oases for tourists in the California Mission Style such as the Las Vegas Castaneda Hotel of 1898 and the Albuquerque Alvarado Hotel of 1901 (demolished in 1970). Within a few years after the turn of the century, Raton, Santa Fe, and Socorro would also boast Mission Revival-style railroad depots and associated buildings.

It is a fascinating cycle of history and fashion that the Mission style and Arts and Crafts aesthetic are in vogue once again in the 1990s. Though the style never completely disappeared, the Mission style was scorned (along

Tucson's Hotel Congress was built in 1919 to provide an oasis for the passengers of the Southern Pacific Railroad. Here the lobby is graced by Arroyo Design's upholstered bench with walnut feet and a generous Mission settle.

with other historical traditions) during the forties, fifties, and sixties by modernist arbiters of design and good taste. The heavy oak Mission furniture appeared too somber and cumbersome in space-age, machine-aesthetic interiors.

Modernism's long reign gave way more than a decade ago to a revival of interest in handcrafted products, vibrant use of colors, natural materials and textures, and an appreciation of Third World ethnic designs and products that helped launch the Santa Fe design boom of the 1980s.

While Santa Fe style still rages in the 1990s, although considered passé

in many circles, the Mission and Arts and Crafts products have been elevated to popular favor and are the subject of scholarly interest. *American Bungalow* magazine is a new publication devoted to Arts and Crafts houses and design, and recent major retrospective exhibitions at the Oakland Museum and the Palm Springs Desert Museum have also heightened interest and public awareness.

The Mission style seems well suited to the sensibilities of the 1990s. Whereas the glamorous, glitzy 1980s espoused a lifestyle of excess, ostentatious wealth, and consumer

A new armchair by the Santa Fe studio of Berkeley Mills gestures to the Southwest by its subtle stepped-cloud design in the back crest and front rail. The upholstery fabric is also inspired by the current wealth of ethnic fabrics in Rio Grande design.

faddishness, the 1990s favor a more earthy and sober lifestyle. Sensible living, practical, well-made products, and a consciousness of environmental protection and Earth Watch causes related the Mission style to contemporary values.

The champions of the original Arts and Crafts and Mission styles, architects such as California's Greene and Greene brothers, Frank Lloyd Wright, and designer Gustav Stickley among them, based their furniture and arch-itectural designs on a fundamental belief that the family and harmonious domestic life had the power to reform society. Products for the home, such as lighting, textiles, ceramics, and fine art should espouse natural designs, materials, and colors. Above all, these products should manifest the highest qualities of honest labor and craftsmanship.

Mission- and Arts and Crafts-style homes (also known as bungalows) and

furniture have a simple, stripped down, elegant appeal, in direct contrast to the ornate and sometimes frivolous Victorian aesthetic. Mission bungalows featured larger family and dining rooms, parlors, and kitchens, interlocked for a free flow of movement and social interaction. The open floor plans of modern houses are derived from the innovations of the Arts and Crafts movement.

Early twentieth-century architects and furniture makers in New Mexico were heavily influenced by the Mission Revival style. The New Mexico Territory's preeminent architects at the turn of the century, brothers Isaac Hamilton Rapp and William Morris Rapp, adapted the Mission style into their eclectic repertoire.

By 1930, entire neighborhoods of California bungalows lined the streets of New Mexico's major towns. In most cases, these cozy homes have been well cared for and preserved, offering attractive lifestyle and home ownership opportunities for today's baby boom generation.

An entire industry of furniture and home accessories based on the Mission style flourished for several decades at the turn of the century. Historic Mission-style furniture is linear, streamlined, elegant, sturdy (sometimes massive), and fashioned of darkened, stained oak. It is usually upholstered with brown or black leather or a pleasing, embroidered textile.

Mission-style cabinets feature

copper or brass hardware, latches, and handles. Glass-faced book and china cabinets are common, as well as inlaid tile sideboards or buffets. In rare and valuable examples, inlaid floral designs of ebony, ivory, or other precious material graces a Mission chest or table.

Hammered copper lamps with stained glass shades, and simple ceramic urns and vases glazed with subdued colors accented the furniture. Southwest Indian pottery and Navajo weavings were prized in a Mission-style interior as examples of pure, handcrafted design. Wicker furniture and lace curtains were also common Mission decorative highlights.

At the height of the Mission style's popularity, New Mexico furniture designers began to adapt Arts and Crafts techniques and forms to the traditional Spanish Colonial aesthetic. Perhaps the most significant legacy of the Mission Revival era for New Mexican interiors is the so-called Taos bed, an oversized deep lounge or settee. Many contemporary Southwestern furniture makers manufacture a Taos bed with unmistakable Mission-style pedigree.

Talented New Mexico furniture makers of the 1920s and 1930s, such as Jesse Nusbaum and William Penhallow Henderson, incorporated Arts and Crafts qualities in their interpretations of Spanish Colonial furniture, such as extending the tenon (or male part of a socket) of a wood joint and enlarging the proportions in the

manner of the majestic Craftsman Morris chair. Nusbaum's furniture for the Museum of Fine Arts in 1920s Santa Fe still has a classic Craftsman-style appeal.

It is not surprising, therefore, that New Mexico would be a hotbed for the Mission Revival of the 1990s. Santa Fe is home to no fewer than three well-known, Mission-style furniture companies. Of these, master craftsman Randolph Laub has developed a prestigious clientele of connoisseurs and movie stars for his graceful furniture and picture frames. Laub's furniture is distinguished by smoothly rounded edges and harmonious proportions.

Berkeley Mills, a California company,

Jesse L. Nusbaum

Besides having a career as an amateur archaeologist and photographer, Jesse L. Nusbaum designed furniture. This Mission-style desk was crafted by Nusbaum for his manual arts class at New Mexico Normal School (now New Mexico Highlands University) in 1908.

Chaparral Studio's sideboard/sofa table displays the new Mission-style preference for curved elements in the overall design. The central, squarish drawer provides dynamic visual tension in this carefully proportioned piece.

has recently established an office and studio in Santa Fe. Their Mission furniture line is inventive and handsomely tapered. Chaparral Studios has introduced a line of mahogany Mission furniture with warm, reddish coloring and a sense of classical styling. All Santa Fe companies offer more exotic and beautiful hardwoods than the traditional Mission oak, and ebony is a popular accent or inlay.

Santa Fe Mission furniture of the 1990s offers a more pleasing palette than the past, and graceful curves of taper, bracing, or profile give the forms a more dynamic stance. The rigid Mission style of the 1920s has given way to an aerodynamic sensibility, much as the Model T was the forerunner of the Ford Taurus.

ON THE CREATIVE METHOD . . . *"I'd eventually like to move to an approach I call 'concept as custom,' meaning that I'm able to conceptualize ideas with a client, do a thumbnail sketch of a project with the client, and go out and build a fantastic piece of furniture.*

"I imagine that this is the way it's always been with great furniture design. I can just see Thomas Chippendale inventing a new highboy with a broken pediment to suit a client's needs...

"It must have been really exciting here in New Mexico around 1850 when the first moldings and new tools arrived. I love to think of this transitional time (in New Mexico) when the old carpenters got this great stuff and just started playing and inventing new furniture. That's the kind of spirit I want to approach in my work. I call that period (in the late nineteenth century) 'cartoon Victorian' or 'naive postmodernism,' but it was really a wonderful time, and we're still studying the pieces that came out of the mix of Spanish Colonial and American influence. It's that sense of exciting and naive invention that I'm aiming for. . . ."

STEVEN PINO, CHAPARRAL FURNITURE

**CHAPARRAL STUDIOS
SANTA FE, NEW MEXICO**

Red mahogany gives Chaparral Studio's bedroom ensemble a distinctive warm glow, which harmonizes well with the Rio Grande's adobe architecture. The spindle bed avoids a heavy feeling by using lean proportions and minimal ornamentation.

Originally based in New York, Stephen Pino's design career has made a transition from streamlined taste to ornate and back to fine elegance of the Arts and Crafts style. Pino is the owner and designer of Chaparral Studios, a Santa Fe company at the vanguard of the current revival of Arts and Crafts or Mission style in the Southwest. Pino's Chaparral line is easily identified by its slender proportions and reddish mahogany color.

Gustav Stickley

An Arroyo Design's
Morris chair is
similar to the
original designed by
Gustav Stickley in
1906; here, it's
crafted of mesquite.

Berkeley Mills is one of those rare furniture companies that is able to synthesize stylistic influence from different cultures and aesthetic traditions. Founded in Berkeley by Dave Kent and Gene Agress, Berkeley Mills adapted the construction techniques of Japanese Tansu furniture and married it to Arts and Crafts styling. The company has also produced cabinets with Shaker-style simplicity.

About 1991, the company established a branch studio in Santa Fe. Spanish Colonial and Pueblo design motifs are making a subtle entry into Berkeley Mills' unique repertoire. Unique and beautifully grained woods characterize Berkeley Mills furniture, as well as simple, pure design.

A prairie table evokes the memory of Frank Lloyd Wright, and Berkeley Mills's straightback chairs borrow a vertical profile from the great Scottish designer Charles Rennie Mackintosh.

ON STYLE . . . *"The technology we have today enables us to make things differently. . . . The traditional Mission-style furniture, to me, lacks softness. I like to bring sensible curves to the Mission style, which also translates to comfort, such as lumbar support.*

"I feel that today's technology, such as more evolved tools and also knowledge of wood, gives us more tools as designers. The superior joinery we can achieve today means that we can use exposed joinery as a design element.

"Berkeley Mills has been in the Southwest for a few years now, and we're responding to local design elements, such as the simplicity of traditional New Mexican furniture and also simple, stepped designs that were ultimately derived from the landscape. . . .

"We've made a new chair that I would call 'Southwest Bauhaus' because of its modern, squarish elements, and this might be a new style for our firm. I can see that we're using more metal and leather, and chrome might become a new material for us to use. . . ."

DAVE KENT, BERKELEY MILLS STUDIO

Randolph Laub demonstrates the compatibility of the Mission and Craftsmen styles with progressive Southwestern architecture in a house he crafted recently near Santa Fe.

Randolph Laub is one of the true artists of the Arts and Crafts style and its philosophy. Growing up in Southern California, Randolph was attracted by the simple nobility of the architecture and furniture of Greene and Greene, and began a career of studying the Arts and Crafts tradition.

Laub moved his studio to Santa Fe in the early 1980s and soon attracted a regional and national reputation for his fine furniture and picture frames (he is known as one of the country's best framers of museum-quality photographs and fine art). Expanding his employees and production rapidly because of his reputation and success, Randolph recently scaled back his studio, now personally crafting and supervising each custom order.

Of his work, Laub follows Mies Van der Rohe's famous dictum that "God is in the details." In Randolph's interpretation, "When you have only a few construction details (in Craftsmen furniture), they should be beautifully and perfectly executed."

Randolph Laub's Craftsmen-style settle is solid and massive, yet its simple styling and lack of ornamentation has a modern appeal.

The Pueblo Deco style of the Hotel Congress provides a striking and colorful environment for a table and chair ensemble by Arroyo Design. The Pasadena chairs, crafted of mesquite and ironwood, are faithful recreations of chairs designed by Greene and Greene for the Blacker House in Pasadena.

Stephen and Elaine Paul have created a unique and sophisti- cated furniture company in Tucson called Arroyo Design. Its three major lines—the Presidio, Mission, and Biedermeier— evoke the history of the Old West and Old World influences as well.

The Presidio Collection is based upon simplified Victorian styles that evolved in the West following the arrival of the railroads after 1870. Arroyo Design's Mission furniture is heavily influenced by the striking joinery techniques first employed by the architecture and furniture of Charles and Henry Greene of Pasadena. The Biedermeier line is classic and stately, a style first created in Germany after the Napoleonic Wars and popular from 1815 to 1848. German immigrants eventually brought their taste for Biedermeier style to the Southwestern frontier, and now Arroyo Design is reviving it in Arizona.

A major distinguishing feature of Arroyo Design's work is its use of mesquite, a desert hardwood tree. Harder than oak, mesquite has a wild and dark grain due to the extreme climate where it flourishes. Often considered a poor wood for anything but firewood, mesquite is championed by Arroyo Design as an attractive, decorative wood and also in consideration of ecology and wiser use of nat- ural products, especially wood.

A detail of Arroyo Design's Mack table reveals the influence of Greene and Greene in the cutout designs and Charles Rennie Mackintosh's proportions.

COWBOY AND RANCH STYLE

Lenore Mulligan and L. D. Burke represent two poles of artistic expression and personality in Rio Grande Cowboy and Ranch style. Burke is a Chicago city slicker who moved to Santa Fe to become a post-modern cowboy, and Lenore (Lopez) Mulligan is a native of the small railroad boomtown of Las Vegas, New Mexico, who went to Hollywood to become a star.

THE NEW COWBOY DESIGNERS

Lenore Mulligan's Cowboy Collection, of Beverly Hills and Santa Fe, features plush furniture uphol-stered in fine western and imported leathers. These "Cowboy Cuddle" chairs and ottoman are at home beneath a Santa Fe hearth. The matching leather mirror and screen are also part of the Cowboy Collection.

Cowboy furniture designer L. D. Burke has developed a highly personal and whimsical style displayed to perfection in his "custom" trastero. Burke embellishes his furniture with witty sayings, cowboy artifacts, and humorous details.

Both have a sense of fun and fantasy and ambition as wide as the Rio Grande itself, which probably explains their success.

Burke is well known for his outrageous furniture style, which evolved out of an exhibit he saw in 1983 at Santa Fe's Museum of International Folk Art, called Carpinteros and Cabinetmakers of New Mexico. L. D. Burke saw that he could create a niche for himself in Southwestern furniture and has since evolved a personal aesthetic, much admired and copied. Burke has managed to condense popular western fantasies, color, artifacts, and personalities into *tour de force* wooden artworks. Images of Billy the Kid, Sitting Bull, Buffalo Bill Cody, and other legends are complemented by actual rifles, spurs, chaps, and similar artifacts attached to the cabinets. Humorous aphorisms pounded out with nail heads on the furniture is another Burke trademark.

While Burke's work represents the pop-culture, *Silverado* aspect that many expect of Santa Fe-based, Rio Grande furniture, Lenore Mulligan's Cowboy Collection represents the sophisticated glamour of Beverly Hills and Rodeo Drive. Mulligan's sofa and club chair designs are covered in sumptuous leathers, built to please the taste of cattle and oil barons.

Lenore admits that she was spoiled by her father and brothers (she was the only girl), and all members of the Lopez clan have developed arts and crafts careers, helping each other along the way. Growing up as a young girl in Las Vegas, just over the Pecos wilderness from Santa Fe, Lenore was fascinated with the town's towering Victorian mansions and also the great Rough Riders Reunion parades and rodeos. Her Teddy Roosevelt chairs pay homage to the great Rough Riders of New Mexico who helped win the Spanish American War nearly a century ago.

Recently, Rio Grande Cowboy and Ranch style has grown dramatically to influence other nearby designers, such as the Texas longhorn furniture makers and the Rustic craftsmen of the Rockies. What was once a curious souvenir or kitschy ornament, Rio Grande Cowboy furniture is now serious business.

Naturalist Home Furnishings of Provo, Utah, produces a handsome saddle-back chair that combines the tooled saddle-leather tradition of Rio Grande Country with a rustic, Rocky Mountain wooden frame.

RIO GRANDE COWBOYS

After the long-awaited opening of the Southwestern frontier, first by Missouri traders who blazed the Santa Fe Trail in 1821 and later by the U.S. Army after the Mexican War in 1848, Rio Grande home style began to change. Good tools and such luxuries as nails, glue, and paint began to transform the old Spanish Colonial furniture.

Imported American furnishings, such as beds, linens, rugs, glassware, and the cherished luxury of piano music transformed New Mexican lifestyles. New Mexican carpinteros began to emulate Yankee furniture and improvise charming new "folk" varia-tions of such foreign styles as Empire, Eastlake, and Queen Anne.

More importantly, the U.S. Army built several large forts in New Mexico and the Southwest to protect the Santa Fe Trail trade and future anticipated rail-road lines. The forts were also essential to quell the "Indian problem" created by the Navajos, Apaches, and Comanches. The presence of forts enabled new com-munities to be founded on the perime-ter of the Rio Grande watershed and attracted cattlemen to New Mexico's substantial rangelands, especially those on the eastern plains near Texas that were watered by the Pecos River.

New Mexico was long familiar with

L. D. Burke's studio and sales gallery are located in a neo-Mission-style building he designed, also affectionately known as the "Pink Church on Pacheco Street" in Santa Fe.

the cattle industry as the Spanish vaquero and Mexican charro preceded the American cowboy on the Southwestern range. Spanish vaqueros developed such well-known cowboy fashions as the big hat, boots, spurs, chaps, and even the classic western stock saddle.

Before the Cowboy and Ranch style became a glamorous product of American popular culture, it emerged and developed as a lifestyle of survival and resourcefulness. Rio Grande ranch style, being the granddaddy of American Western ranch style, is naturally rooted in the Spanish haciendas of New Mexico. The interiors of simple adobe houses were very sparsely furnished with a few hand-hewn chairs, a table, chest, and perhaps a trastero. Buffalo, sheep, and other animal hides were laid on earthen floors at night to provide a place to sleep.

Haciendas and ranch compounds were often adapted to the livestock. Adobe and stone walls attached to and surrounding the house provided a safe haven in case of Indian attack, and heavy *zaguan* doors allowed access for carriages and wagons. New Mexican ranches used available sandstone, also called flagstone or ledgestone, for rustic houses, fireplaces, stables, and storage buildings, most notably in the upper Pecos River valley villages such as San Jose and Villanueva. These villages were founded during the late Spanish Colonial and Mexican periods from 1800 to 1820 and are located about thirty miles southeast of Santa Fe. In higher locations above the Rio Grande, rounded river rocks and mountain stones are combined with logs to fashion cozy ranch houses and cottages for summer dude ranches.

▲

A generous
Cowboy cupboard
by Cowboy Classics
is a distinctive
masterpiece
embodying the
lodgepole tradition
but adding a
cowboy flavor with
horseshoe drawer
pulls and carved
silhouette at the top.

▼

◄ A dining chair made by Cowboy Classics' Tom Bice of Longmont, Colorado, is inspired by the Cody style developed by Thomas Molesworth and a new generation of western designers. ▼

Milo Marks ▼

▲ A massive heirloom armoire is adorned by carved cattle-brand symbols. Marks's longhorn table in front features a clever and charming barbed-wire border on the table skirts.

New Mexico has contributed mightily to the legend and mystique of the Old West. Such famous western icons

CLASSIC RIO GRANDE COWBOY STYLE

as Geronimo, Kit Carson, Billy the Kid, Doc Holliday, and Manuelito roamed near the Rio Grande in their heyday. Cattle ranching is still one of the state's major industries, and nearly every community sponsors a rodeo, from small villages such as Wagon Mound to Albuquerque's grand finale at the State Fair.

The Rio Grande Cowboy style has tended to remain true to New Mexico's own design traditions rather than espouse other classic Cowboy looks such as the Texas longhorn furniture or the northern Cowboy style developed by Thomas Molesworth in Cody, Wyoming. Working ranches, dude ranches, and log cabin retreats of New Mexico's high country are usually crafted of large, ponderosa pine, tree trunks and have a massive, rustic appeal. The living room of the Gascon Ranch, located near the soaring Truchas Peaks of Mora County, still retains much of its original 1920s ranch decor.

Editha Bartley operates the ranch, a veritable Shangri-la located at the end of a winding dirt road, which unfolds past small adobe cottages emitting tassels of white smoke, even in early summer.

The main ranch house was built about 1885 and is the heart of a rambling complex of barns, cabins, and stables. A first impression of the living

room is that of a Hollywood movie set, and one could easily picture Ben Cartwright of *Bonanza* at home here, reading a book by the fire.

The room's contents are authentic and thus an early expression of Rio Grande Cowboy style. The back wall is branded with the irons of surrounding ranches. The Pueblo pottery on the mantel is all antique, dating from the 1920s, as are all the splendid Navajo rugs on the floor and chairs. The wicker sofas are in good repair. Antique firearms, brass standing lamps, and horseshoe fireplace accessories contribute to the ranch ambience.

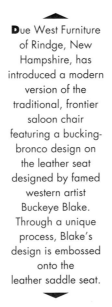

Icons of the Old West are proudly featured on L. D. Burke's cabinets, such as miniature buffalo roaming freely beneath a majestic mountain range atop his "Buffalo" trastero.

Due West Furniture of Rindge, New Hampshire, has introduced a modern version of the traditional, frontier saloon chair featuring a bucking-bronco design on the leather seat designed by famed western artist Buckeye Blake. Through a unique process, Blake's design is embossed onto the leather saddle seat.

East of the Rio Grande, on the vast flatlands of Texas, the modern cattle industry was developed on such legendary spreads as the King Ranch. Here, the famed Texas longhorns flourished. Milo Marks grew up in this cowboy paradise near Houston, learning cowboy business and lore from his grandfather, E. H. Marks.

Today, Milo and his wife, Teddi, have risen to the top of the western cowboy furniture industry on the merit of Milo's exceptional craftsmanship and Teddi's design and marketing skills. Teddi's long involvement in the antiques industry has given her a unique sense of history and western tradition.

Milo's Western Heritage Design Collection is distinctively Texan, as it proudly employs the use of longhorns, carefully polished and reinforced, for structural cabinet and table legs. Longhorn furniture was among the West's first distinctive furniture styles, popular in Texas ranch homes and collected for East Coast parlors and offices as souvenirs after 1880.

Milo's classic, Texas furniture line skyrocketed after it was introduced at cutting-horse shows in Texas a few years ago. "Our friends wanted it for their ranches, and pretty soon we couldn't keep up with the orders," Teddi recalls.

The couple also developed a line of cabinets, chest of drawers, and armoires to complement the longhorn look. Milo's cabinets feature a lovely, overall, textural effect made by careful chisel-gouging, and carved-relief effects such as Texas Lone Stars, barbed wire, cattle brands, and horseshoes.

Longhorns have been a traditional accent for Texas ranch furniture since the nineteenth century. No other contemporary western furniture maker uses them as dramatically as Milo Marks, Meridian, Texas.

LENORE MULLIGAN
COWBOY COLLECTION

**SANTA FE, NEW MEXICO, AND
BEVERLY HILLS, CALIFORNIA**

Born and raised in Las Vegas, New Mexico, Lenore Mulligan was spoiled by her father and three brothers. This taught her a thing or two about what men like. Now, with her posh Cowboy Collection of leather furniture, Lenore has designed seating with a masculine appeal and Fifth Avenue styling.

Working as an interior designer in Los Angeles, Lenore couldn't quite find the sumptuous look of the Old West required by some of her clients, so she decided to create it. Back in 1991, Lenore took her new collection to Santa Fe and sold it to local furniture boutiques off the truck. Now her Cowboy Collection is found in forty-seven designer showrooms across the country.

Lenore loves being part of the renaissance in contemporary western furniture, observing that "much of today's furniture is already classic." The romance of hide and leather products is part of the western aura, and Lenore is proud to offer furniture crafted of the finest leather.

"I use 'naked' hides as opposed to 'raw' hides. Naked hides are processed to feel almost like supple deer hide. They breathe and acquire a wonderful patina with age," she notes.

Lenore claims that many men sit in the furniture and don't want to get up, sometimes writing a check for the sofa on the spot. "My furniture is designed with a woman's sense of design appeal and a man's standard of generous comfort," Lenore says proudly.

A condo at Santa Fe's Quail Run complex is styled by Lenore Mulligan's Cowboy Collection. "Teddy Roosevelt" chairs have Eastlake-style frames and plush velvet upholstery. The Southwest sofa features a Corona blanket fabric.

A Cowboy
Collection display
by Lenore Mulligan
includes a horned
mirror, a boot
wreath, a Southwest
whipstitched-leather
sofa, and a leather
wing chair

Cowboy and Ranch furnishings with a distinctive Rio Grande look did not appear until the mid-1980s, when designer L. D. Burke III discovered New Mexican furniture displayed at the seminal Carpinteros and Cabinet-makers exhibit at the Museum of International Folk Art, featuring curators Lonn Taylor and Dessa Bokides (November 1983–April 1984).

"I found the stuff incredibly naive, charming, and beautiful, and I looked at the marketplace and didn't think anyone was making a very good translation," L. D. recalls. "I knew it would be boring to just copy others, so I began taking the historic pieces as a starting point to create contemporary derivatives of New Mexican furniture."

▲ **A** variation on Woodwright's "Western Boot" cupboard celebrates a Native American theme with strong turquoise color and stepped-design accents. ▼

Burke's style has evolved to a true cowboy image, often incorporating actual cowboy artifacts such as boots, spurs, buckles, guns, and horns as decorative accents on the furniture. A lingering trace of the Hispanic cabinetry tradition is still evident in some of his larger trasteros, but Burke's pieces are distinctive and original.

Old western culture captured the imagination of nearly everyone after the phenomenal success of *Dances With Wolves*, and designers along the Rio Grande were quick to respond with exciting new furnishings. Large leather sofas and chairs have become an instant classic of Rio Grande high style, and several designers have created compelling western variations.

The Elizabeth Drey Collection of Santa Fe offers large leather sofas and chairs ornamented with classic fringed tassels, handpainted border designs, and silver conchos. Lenore Mulligan's Cowboy Collection of Santa Fe and Beverly Hills features a sophisticated *Urban Cowboy* personality, incorporating a wide variety of leathers and upholstery, including colored and natural suedes, tooled and hand-stitched leather, Pendleton and Chimayo fabrics. Cassandra Lohr's Old West Collection features a natural, yellow, elk-hide sofa.

Other designers and studios are introducing new materials and combining others to achieve dramatic new visual effects. Woodwright Furniture of Santa Fe is juxtaposing country cabinetry with tooled saddle leather inserts and borders. Mike Livingston of Hutchinson, Kansas, carves masterful cabinets featuring some rope motifs, boot and barbed-wire hardware. Cowboy Classics of Longmont, Colorado, offers rugged log and lodgepole furniture accented by horseshoe drawer pulls, some Molesworth-carved motifs, and tooled saddle leather.

Lenore Mulligan

A southwestern club chair from Lenore Mulligan's Cowboy Collection is given a distinctively western personality by its Pendleton blanket upholstery.

Cassandra Lohr's
Old West Collection
of Aspen offers a
matching set of
western, hand-carved
gun desk and chairs.

JACE ROMICK
STEAMBOAT SPRINGS, COLORADO

Jace Romick is equally at home screaming down the ski slopes, or riding a wild bronco, or crafting a great western cabinet. Romick's gallery, Into the West, located in Steamboat Springs, showcases his own distinctive line of Cowboy lodgepole furniture along with other Cowboy and Ranch collectibles.

Romick has successfully blended the rustic appeal of mountain lodgepole design with classic leather and hide effects. Tooled saddle leather and raw cowhide give Romick's line a dramatic, picturesque character. Combined with cowboy-patterned textiles and innovative touches such as silver and leather concho pulls, the overall effect is rugged and masculine.

An armoire by Jace Romick's Lodgepole Furniture Company of Steamboat

L. D. Burke's "Green" trastero is a formal and symmetrical cabinet design, carefully proportioned and displaying an interesting arrangement of drawers and panels. Otherwise, the piece is a Wild West fantasy that Burke is well known for.

MIKE LIVINGSTON
HUTCHINSON, KANSAS

Cowboy style is not exactly descriptive of Mike Livingston's unique furniture, although Livingston's furniture has found a popular niche in Rio Grande home design. Livingston's approach to western furniture combines Old World romanticism, some favorite Spanish religious icons, and Yankee pragmatism.

Trained as a sculptor, Livingston is careful to endow his pieces with rich textural effects and superbly carved reliefs. Mike borrows popular symbols such as rosettes and angel cherubs from the Spanish Colonial tradition, yet also enjoys popular cowboy accents, such as a painted bronc buster and handmade, bronze hardware in the form of cowboy boots and barbed wire. The cabinetry design is simple and refined and sturdily pegged together.

An artist of Mike's caliber is surely a tribute to his Hutchinson, Kansas, hometown. Livingston's design philosophy is succinct and powerful: "To me, evidence of the hand(work) is all important."

Mike Livingston's furniture reveals the fine eye and hand of a master sculptor and craftsman. This charming nightstand is graced by a cherub and the carved saying "One is the architect of one's own destiny."

NATIVE AMERICAN VISIONS

Furniture is at heart an Old World concept. People in the New World preferred (or for lack of technology) sitting and sleeping on the ground, surrounded by natural, handmade products essential for daily living. Today only Zuni Pueblo in western New Mexico, one of the West's oldest and best preserved cultures, is producing unique Native American furniture of the Southwest.

The interior of a tepee near Aspen designed by Cassandra Lohr is inviting, with a yellow, cowhide sofa, a New Mexican Spanish Colonial chest/table, Navajo rugs, and other Native American ornamental items.

In the old Zuni mission of Nuestra Senora de Guadalupe, built in 1629, magnificently carved corbels shoulder the weight of splendid *vigas* (heavy, wooden roof beams), a lasting testimony to the excellent carpentry once practiced in the village. Like a prodigal child, fine carpentry and furniture making have returned to Zuni Pueblo after an absence of many years, pehaps centuries. The Zuni Furniture Enterprise is an innovative, economic-development project that is training young craftsmen in the art of furniture making.

Furniture making and architectural woodwork are fundamentally foreign concepts in the Pueblo world. In traditional Pueblo architecture, places to sit or store things are built organically into the walls as bancos or nichos. Doors, window frames, and ladders provide some opportunities for expression, but original examples of Zuni carpentry are rare.

Since there is really no aesthetic precedent for Zuni—or Pueblo—furni-

ture of indigenous design, the program has experimented with various joinery and finishing techniques. Traditional Spanish Colonial and Southwestern furniture technology such as mortise-and-tenon joinery became a foundation for later innovation such as chip carving and sandblasting. The original group of craftsmen also learned how to design and paint traditional Zuni figures on furniture, such as the rain bird and the deer with heartline.

Soon, influences from the Spanish Colonial and the Zuni world combined into a new style. It was inevitable that one of Zuni's trademark products—carved fetish figures—would be incorporated into the furniture. Now, painted benches with carved animal figures

West By Southwest's "Running Stallion" settee.

West By
Southwest's
bedroom is
both colorful
and whimsical.

are among the program's most popular items.

Represented by retail stores in exclusive shopping districts of San Francisco and Los Angeles, Zuni Pueblo continues to refine its trading tradition. As many as five or six centuries ago, the isolated western pueblos imported seashells from the Pacific coast and macaw feathers from Mexico. Today, Zuni is one of only three Native American tribes, along with the Yakimas of Washington and the Cherokees of North Carolina, producing furniture.

A dramatic leather
chair designed by
Lester Santos for the
Sweetwater Ranch
Collection of Cody,
Wyoming, interprets
the Plains Indian
tradition of painting
memorable life
scenes on ledger
paper or hides.

Santa Fe's Southwest
Spanish Craftsmen
features a unique,
round, coffee table
painted with
Acoma-style, Pueblo
pottery designs.

ZUNI FURNITURE ENTERPRISE
ZUNI PUEBLO, NEW MEXICO

Zuni Pueblo is among the most ancient of American communities, having been settled for about seven centuries. Located thirty miles south of Gallup, New Mexico, Zuni is the largest Pueblo, housing about 7,000 people.

Zuni's unique culture, language, and artistic traditions are the source of endless scholarly and popular fascination. So it is remarkable that the tribe has begun producing its own special line of furniture.

Zuni was the site of the first fateful encounter between Coronado's expedition of 1540 and a Southwestern Native American culture. Throughout the long Spanish Colonial period, which ended with Mexican Independence in 1821, Pueblo craftsmen were trained in carpentry, blacksmithing, and building construction; but not until Zuni's furniture enterprise, which began in 1991, has a Southwestern tribe produced its own furniture based on Native American designs.

Zuni furniture is adorned with painted and carved representations of sacred animals and spiritual beings called *kachinas*. Border and decorative designs are also derived from pottery and weaving motifs.

Ancient Zuni Pueblo, located thirty miles south of Gallup, New Mexico, recently introduced a line of furniture adorned by traditional, painted pottery designs.

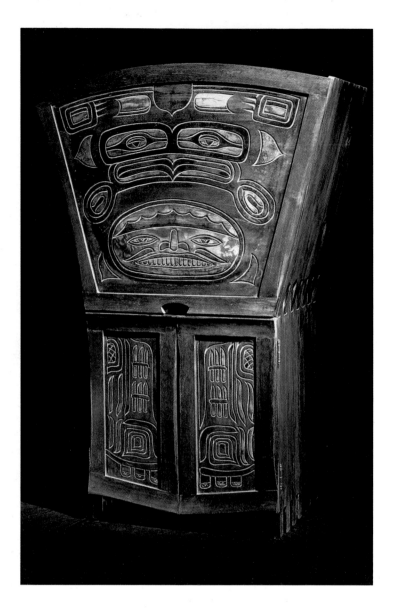

Jeremy Morrelli freely borrows and interprets designs from native and western cultures, such as Chippendale, and is one of the masters of expressing Native American images on contemporary cabinets. This unusual armoire boldly displays carvings from the Pacific Northwest culture.

Native Americans for at least 15,000 years, and some of the earliest known human remains of Folsom Man and Sandia Man were found in Rio Grande country. More familiar are the spectacular ruins and homesites of the Anasazi people at sites such as Mesa Verde and Chaco Canyon, the remains of the Hohokam clans of southern Arizona, and the pottery left behind by the Mimbres culture of southwestern New Mexico. The petroglyph drawings of these people on isolated rock outcroppings, along with their pottery designs and paintings on kiva walls, are a rich heritage of designs for contemporary furniture makers.

A few centuries before the first Spanish colonists appeared in the Southwest, when tribes of people migrated in all directions in search of water and dependable food supplies, new cultures began to develop. A severe drought in the thirteenth century (along with other factors) forced many people from the Four Corners region into the immediate vicinity of the Rio Grande, where new pueblos were built. Between the tenth and thirteenth centuries, the Navajos descended from

The Rio Grande watershed and the greater Four Corners region of the Southwest boast a dynamic legacy of Native American cultures, perhaps the best preserved in the United States. Though long appreciated by art connoisseurs, Southwestern Native American design is only now fully emerging as an appealing style or decorative motif for furniture.

The Rio Grande has nourished

A RICH TAPESTRY OF DESIGN

Sculptural form is at the heart of John Bauer's work. The Santa Fe resident has been producing high-quality furniture for twenty years and claims that "similarities to traditional designs (in my work) occur because of function and not from drawing on historic furniture forms."

Recently, however, Bauer's work has featured a fascinating homage to the southwest's Native American people and cultures. In his southwestern figure chairs, Native American historical figures are carved into the backs of the chairs in remarkable, historical accuracy.

Bauer's method is to research photographic archives to select an appropriate image. Apache scouts photographed by the U.S. Army at the turn of the century and Navajo portraits by famed photographer A. C. Vroman have rematerialized on Bauer's chairs. John is also fond of Mimbres pottery designs, and these also appear as inlaid motifs on his furniture.

Through the highly polished and carved surfaces of his furniture and various imagery and symbolism of his themes, John Bauer aims to touch the viewers' unconscious realm.

▲

John Bauer of Santa Fe preserves the memory of turn-of-the-century Navajo figures in his Navajo chair. Based on photographs taken by A. C. Vroman, the male figure on the left is dressed to attend the 1903 Pasadena Tournament of Roses Parade. He is wearing a leather horned hat. The inlaid medallion on the back is inspired by a Navajo rug design.

▼

California Handmade's petroglyph table.

the western Rocky Mountains and plains of Canada into a large area of northern Arizona and northwestern New Mexico.

Other wandering tribes eked out an existence in the harsh environment of the high desert until the Spanish bounty of horses, cattle, and sheep changed economic opportunities for Rio Grande tribes after 1600. The Navajos, the Utes of southern Colorado, the Comanches, Kiowas, and Apaches of the eastern mountains and plains rose to prominence and cultural self-realization as a consequence of mobility provided by horses.

The Spaniards contributed other important technologies to southwestern tribes (especially the Navajo), including weaving and silversmithing. Pueblo craftsmen were trained in carpentry and blacksmithing at several Pueblos, and thus some Pueblo designs, such as the stepped-cloud image, appeared on early colonial furniture.

As the Spanish Colonial settlements in New Mexico became more established in the eighteenth century, a complex diplomatic system of interdependency and balance of power enabled annual trade fairs at various locations—notably at Taos and Pecos pueblos. Here the trading of raw and finished products helped foster a tradition of cultural interchange that is the dominant quality of Rio Grande high style.

The great hunters of the eastern plains, the Kiowas and Comanches, brought tanned buffalo, elk, and deer hides to trade; the Pueblos bartered corn, pottery, and clothing; and the Spanish offered forged metal tools. Rio Grande designers still freely incorporate these treasures in their designs. The Elizabeth Drey Collection offers easy chairs and sofas in tanned suede leather adorned with Native American designs. Pueblo pottery designs are utilized by several designers, including Southwest Spanish Craftsmen, Gunther Worrlein, and the Zuni Furniture Enterprise.

Santa Fe master craftsman Gunther Worrlein has chosen the elegant and ethereal animal imagery created by the Mimbres culture of Southwestern New Mexico for some of his furniture expressions.

ON TRADITION . . . *"I was trained in Italy, where the guilds are freer (than in Germany) and creative expression is encouraged. Then I moved with my wife to New Orleans, where I carved Chippendale reproductions for several years. When I moved to New Mexico in 1980, I was immediately attracted to Mimbres design. . . . It's impossible not to be attracted by their designs—they're so perfect.*

"I try to elaborate and put my own expression on the traditional styles. Even the Egyptians built upon older traditions. I really appreciate some of the new directions that New Mexico furniture is taking. My work is built upon the traditional, but (it) has my own personality, which likes the grand gesture."

GUNTHER WORRLEIN, WORRLEIN STUDIOS

"Gunther has a baroque heart! . . . but I'm also part of the team. I help finish the pieces and give him advice on the designs."

JOAN WORRLEIN

▲
Elizabeth Drey
▼

Fringed-leather
chairs surround a
suede table adorned
by a painted
variation of a Zuni
rainbird design.
The table by
Elizabeth Drey bears
other Pueblo painted
designs and prayer
feathers on the legs.
A western-style
leather jacket and
throw pillows are
also featured in the
Elizabeth Drey
Collection.

West By Southwest's bathroom fixtures.

Navajo throne chairs by Morrelli incorporate features of Chippendale styling and proportions with Art Deco-carved profiles and Navajo blanket designs.

ELIZABETH DREY
SANTA FE, NEW MEXICO

With an extensive background in world travel and design, Elizabeth Drey made a dramatic entre into the Santa Fe design scene in 1991. Elizabeth was an interior designer in Louisiana for several years before moving to Texas to work for W. J. Sloan Company, where she designed stores and was a product furniture designer.

Searching for a place where she could open a store to sell artifacts collected from her travels, Elizabeth was captivated by Santa Fe and its intriguing cultures. Soon she was inspired to design new Rio Grande furnishings.

"One of my first ideas was the big leather sofa we show in our advertisements. I had scheduled an opening for my store and didn't have much to show," Elizabeth says with a chuckle. "So I bought this expensive sofa in Albuquerque, and we tore it up for five days and managed to cover it in suede. It was a big hit."

The Elizabeth Drey Collection features supple natural leathers adorned with Navajo designs. Most of Elizabeth's production staff is Navajo, and she consults them often for ideas. New Mexico is still new to Elizabeth, and her fascination with it is undiminished. "I love the horses around here! They're a great medium for expression. I definitely want to work more with horses in my new designs."

A custom, leather easy chair and ottoman by Elizabeth Drey of Santa Fe incorporate designs inspired by Navajo rug patterns. Medicine sticks and a Taos-style tom-tom drum complete the ensemble.

John Bauer of Santa Fe utilizes an expressionistic approach to design his Anasazi frog bench. Curving, sensuous, animal-like table legs lead the eye to a magnificent central frog medallion crafted of exotic woods.

Cassandra Lohr, Old West Collection.

Traditionally, Pueblo cultural imagery has been most prevalent in southwest architecture, interior designs, and furniture. Twentieth-century southwestern design has spawned

the appearance of Pueblo Revival and Pueblo Deco architecture, and architects such as John Gaw Meem and Mary Colter were skillful at combining Pueblo motifs with modern carpentry and wrought iron.

Ancient Pueblo pottery designs, especially the enigmatic drawings of the Mimbres people, are being translated into carved features of today's furniture. Petroglyph symbols of the humpbacked flute player, *Kokopelli,* and various sacred animals are being forged in iron and steel.

Navajo designs such as blanket patterns and silver conchos are also appearing as door and chair decorations or as ornaments on cowboy furniture.

Upholstery fabrics based on the Navajo tradition or other Southwestern textiles began to appear in the 1980s and are now commonly accepted by mainstream American furniture manufacturers.

The newest innovations in Native American-inspired furniture of the Rio Grande are arriving from the northern Plains Indian cultures of Colorado and Wyoming. Intricate, beaded, leather work is common among Plains tribes from Canada to Texas. Recently, beaded Reebok tennis shoes from New Mexico caused a ripple in the fashion world, and beaded leather pillows and blankets from Cassandra Lohr's Old West Collection of Aspen continue the tradition.

Santa Fe and Taos art galleries regularly display the famous ledger paintings of Plains Indians of the late nineteenth century, and some contemporary Native American artists employ a ledger-style painting in their works. Sweetwater Ranch Furniture of

Cedar and burled-wood tables by Cassandra Lohr of Aspen are adorned on top by inlaid-tile designs derived from quilts.

Based in Aspen, Cassandra Lohr's Old West Collection represents a collaborative approach to western design. Cassandra's company offers selected products, including beds, desks, chairs, sofas, tables, and credenzas as well as artifacts and accessories hand-crafted by a dozen artisans, many of them Native American.

Her interpretation of a modern tepee for a client's retreat near Aspen was featured on the cover of *Architectural Digest* magazine (August 1994). The tepee represents a symbolic and spiritual shelter for Native Americans, according to Lohr. "Everything Native Americans do is in a circle—their ceremonies, their communities, their tepees—for all life moves in a circle: the end becomes the beginning; the old begins the new."

Describing her unique collection, Cassandra waxes poetic. "The making of these objects is almost a lost art today, because people want things ready-made and ready to go. Manufactured cannot create the beauty and feel of handmade. Factories cannot reproduce the colors from the earth and sky that saturate western sunsets and canyon lands, nor the smell of burnished leather of a well-worn saddle, nor the natural, spontaneous weave of geometric designs on native pottery."

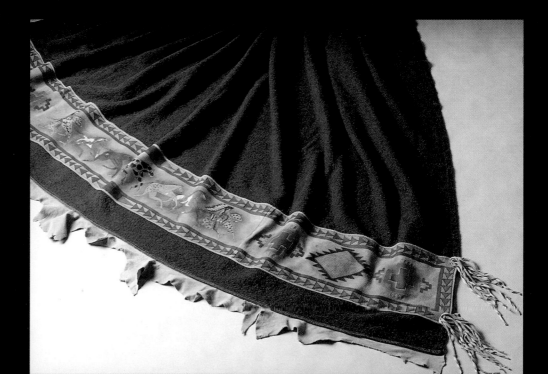

Cassandra Lohr,
Old West Collection.
Hand-painted
blanket.

West By Southwest's Yeii dining room ensemble.

Interior shot of wood bed in Cassandra Lohr tepee.

Cody, Wyoming, has introduced a new chair with ledger-style paintings of Indians on the upholstery. This seems to be a milepost in Native American-inspired furniture design.

Many people these days want to embrace a romanticized version of the Native American lifestyle—but with all the comforts of 1990s technology. A space-age tepee designed as a man's retreat on the edge of a pristine lake in the Colorado Rockies (near Aspen) was furnished by Cassandra Lohr and featured on the cover of *Architectural Digest*'s August 1994 issue.

In Santa Fe, the tony Inn of the Anasazi lures upscale tourists to its interiors boasting Chaco Canyon-style walls of intricately cut and fitted sandstone. Visitors enter the Pueblo Revival castle through Pueblo Deco doors designed and crafted by Jeremy Morelli Studio of Santa Fe.

Still, these inspired expressions of Native American furniture and design are overwhelmingly influenced by professional and non-Native American designers. What does appear to be developing in its very early stages is a spirit of collaboration and consultation whereby some Native American artists are being attracted to furniture design. Appreciation of natural furnishings with tribal-based designs is a growing element of Rio Grande high style. Its potential appeal is limitless when Native American artists and craftsmen begin to transform European and American concepts of furniture and home design and make it their own.

SOVEREIGN NATIVE
GOLDEN, COLORADO

Sovereign Native is a unique art and furnishings company based in Golden, Colorado, and devoted to the expression of Native American design through advanced technology. Owner Douglas Rich jokingly refers to his products as something like what would happen if a "Porsche ran into a tepee."

Since it's the only company producing furniture constructed of carbon fiber and featuring a "seating matrix" that uses a revolutionary new foam material also being employed by NASA, Sovereign Native's look is indeed progressive.

Native American designs inspired by Navajo blanket patterns are produced by using inlaid, exotic, hardwood veneers. Each chair back features a Spirit Line similar to those woven into Navajo rugs.

Douglas Rich embodies some of the pioneering spirit of the Old West by boldly declaring that "the time is right to head in a new direction with Native American/Southwest furniture design. . . . We are employing the latest materials and techniques to produce a more contemporary, lighter look. All art forms evolve, and I feel that my firm is leading the way into a new facet of South-west art."

▲

Sovereign Native's chair design is called "Soft Wind Song." The chair is constructed of carbon fiber and is upholstered with a special, new foam material called HF2 matrix foam. The chair is inlaid with exotic, hardwood veneers to produce a blanket pattern, which also contains a Spirit Line like that found in Navajo weaving.

▼

A magnificent Aztec headboard is a Morrelli original. The headboard is inspired by the colorful headdresses worn by the Aztecs and crafted of exotic, jungle bird feathers such as the quetzal. The feathers surround a hammered copper inset.

A custom doorway by Morrelli Studio elaborates on the Anasazi theme by weaving the blanket design outward to engulf the top transom and sidelight openings.

Santa Fe
New Mexico's
Inn of the Anazazi.
Doors by
Jeremy Morrelli.

Santa Fe designer
Jeremy Morrelli has
produced a striking
set of Anasazi doors
derived from the
ancient Pueblo
tradition of hanging
a colorful blanket in
doorways as a
threshold barrier.
Shown here is
Chief Blanket 5.

Guylyn Durham is the owner of West by Southwest, a furniture and design company based in the Four Corners community of Farmington, New Mexico. The strong presence of ancient Anasazi design and the vitality of Navajo art have influenced Guylyn's furniture.

Guylyn studied under various southwestern artists and developed her own distinctive style. Using as inspiration the petroglyphs, pottery, rugs, and jewelry of the Four Corners region, she has created intriguing, original, steel sculptures and furniture.

When asked about the unique quality of her designs, Durham calls it "originality through isolation." Drawing from the remoteness of her Four Corners environment, she turns to the ancient native artists for inspiration. Guylyn holds these artists in highest esteem for their insight into style, which often projects a contemporary feeling when adapted to steel.

▲
West By Southwest's
Yeii bench.
▼

▲
West By Southwest's
Yeii candleabra.
▼

RIO GRANDE CONTEMPORARY CRAFTSMEN

A large mural on Guadalupe Street in downtown Santa Fe extends a giant hand with an eye nestled in its palm. The all-seeing oracle represents the visionary, and the fingers of the hand are symbolic stages in the career path of the craftsman. Behind the mysterious mural is the remarkable studio and workshop of Jeremy Morrelli, a talented designer of cutting-edge, contemporary, Rio Grande furniture.

Adobe Furniture of Dallas has unveiled a line of furniture inspired by the adobe furniture of the Southwest. Made of a unique "synthetic adobe" process, the pieces appear massive yet are relatively lightweight. The Santa Fe bed represents the stepped design of a Pueblo in front and the flowing natural lines of a mountain range in back.

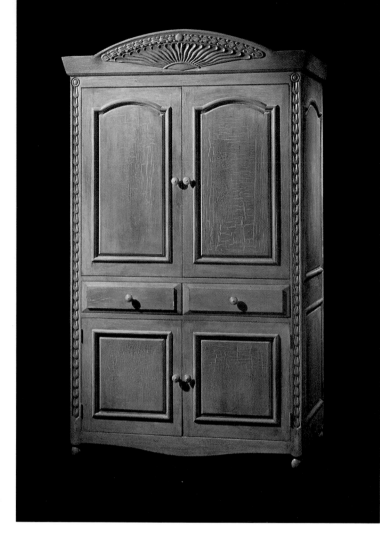

ON THE STUDIO PROCESS . . . *"On the wall of my studio, there's a mural painting of a hand with five fingers outstretched. And these five fingers symbolize the five stages of development of a craftsman. The first finger is the apprentice. Then the apprentice becomes a journeyman. After more training, the journeyman becomes a craftsman. At this stage, the craftsman has mastered all techniques in the studio, but he can't advance until he produces a masterpiece. Then he becomes a master craftsman, the fourth stage. Finally, the thumb or fifth stage is the visionary, whose insight guides the studio and himself.*

"At the base of the hand are three words—Attention, Dexterity, and Confidence—and these are the three qualities of a craftsman.

"What I'm trying to establish in my studio is something like the old guilds (of Europe). The apprentices and journeymen are required to take instruction and demonstrate their skills. The master craftsmen are required to teach what they know on a regular basis. And as the visionary, I'm constantly looking for new design approaches for our work. I've found a rich source of inspiration in the Native American tradition and also the African."

JEREMY MORRELLI, MORRELLI STUDIO

Morrelli epitomizes the neo-southwestern craftsman—thoroughly romantic in a love for the past, eclectic in taste, but progressive in adapting the latest technology to serve the progress of design. Inside the large warehouse-like studio, a noisy drone of tools working and people shuffling about distracts from the magnificent pieces of furniture, hardware, and architectural elements being produced. The styles and forms are dazzling—a Nicolai Fechin carving here and there, Hopi and Navajo designs, stylized natural forms, haunting Native American images from the forests of the Pacific Northwest and the jungles of Aztec Mexico.

It appears to be a seamless design factory, but the large cartoon and pattern drawings are smudged with the toil of pencil errors and rethinking sketches. Morrelli's studio is nothing less than an Old World furniture guild transplanted into New Mexico. Craftsmen at Morrelli move up through the ranks, teaching each other the secrets of design, carving, and joinery. Each craftsman aspires to create a masterpiece, which signals the hard-earned status of a mas-

Ernest Thompson Studio of Albuquerque produces luxurious
armchairs that blend a classical scroll-arm motif with a Pueblo cloud-design
accent. The background mantel and fireplace also demonstrate
the blending of classical style and New Mexico's adobe architecture,
which is becoming popular once again.

Actually, after World War II, American furniture design was dominated by the long shadow of modernism. Great designers such as Eero Saarinen and Charles Eames used modern industrial materials such as chrome and bent plywood, avoiding historical references and ornament. Furniture of the 1950s achieved a refined, machine-like, sculptural quality that appeared futuristic but ultimately was discarded by the public in the 1960s as people sought a new homestyle.

The so-called cultural revolution of the 1960s and the ideal of a free lifestyle based on a return to nature and transcendental experience embodied by the hippies spelled doom for the industrial ideal of modernism. Many young people savored J. R. R. Tolkien's *The Hobbit* during this era, and many tried to recreate (at least in their minds) an idyllic home based on nature and simple craftsmanship.

A large number of pop generation adventurers sought refuge in America's forests, backwoods, villages, and wilderness areas and actively forged a lifestyle based on self-reliance and ingenuity. The largely unspoiled beauty of northern California, upstate New York, and the northern Rio Grande corridor attracted many young people wishing to "tune in and drop out."

Self-help books and guides to alternative building technologies seemed to be everywhere in the 1970s. Led by the *Whole Earth Catalog*, others offered books on building domes and geodesic zomes, solar-energy housing, adobe structures, and even houses made of recycled aluminum cans and tires. Traditional ethnic housing forms such as yurts and tepees became fashionable.

An entire generation of craftsmen has come of age in New Mexico, many self-taught and espousing a design philosophy akin to the Arts and Crafts

ter craftsman. Beyond the skills of a master craftsman, a visionary seeks his unique inspiration and expression. Having established his studio, Jeremy Morrelli can see a new challenge in his immediate future—the integration of architecture, furniture, and interior design, all with a Morrelli signature style.

Besides Jeremy Morrelli, a remarkable number of master craftsmen are working in Rio Grande country, practicing highly personal, contemporary, furniture styles, borrowing freely from the traditions of the past but urgently seeking a progressive, innovative art form. With the sensational recent success of Santa Fe style, Rio Grande furniture design has tended to be stereotyped into a Spanish or cowboy pigeonhole. The fact is that the past twenty years have witnessed the development of a sophisticated contemporary design tradition in New Mexico.

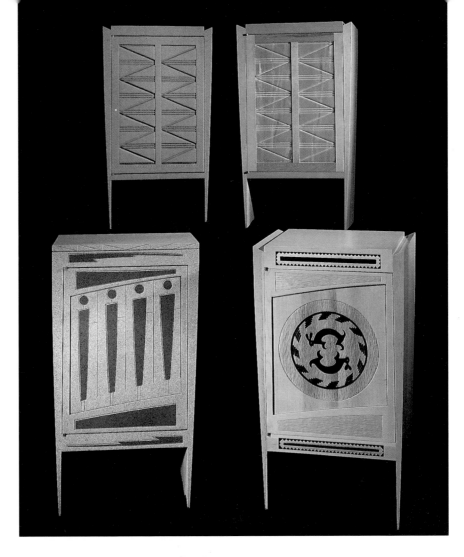

Chris Sandoval's studio, Artisans of the Desert, produces a sensational set of wine cabinets with southwestern Art Deco styling.

Furniture artist David Kozlowski of Santa Fe strives to "create a subtle dynamism that is derived from purity of form and surface." His "Surfin'" sideboard, constructed of mahogany and steel, is a sculptural expression as well as a functional table.

An intimate, kitchen-dining ensemble by Peter Gould incorporates traditional styling elements familiar to New Mexican furniture but also features contemporary touches such as woven seats and strong color.

ideal of simple, functional design, high-quality natural materials, and meticulous craftsmanship. The Contemporary Craftsmen movement of the 1990s in the Southwest is more eclectic in its stylistic influences than the Craftsmen movement of a century ago and employs a broad palette of materials.

Today's Contemporary Craftsmen of the Rio Grande seek inspiration in classical forms—Chippendale, Art Deco, Shaker, and even modernism itself. Though individual craftsmen incorporate their favorite design styles into their work, an appreciation for refined finishes and styling is a common quality cherished by Rio Grande craftsmen. References to historical precedents are subtle in their work. The restrained ornamentation of Rio Grande contemporary furniture is likely a result of the influence of modernism and the advent of high technology.

While the Rio Grande is an ancient homeland, it is by no means constrained by its powerful history. Just a few minutes by automobile from the pueblo cliff dwellings of Puye are the awesome National Laboratories of Los Alamos. Furniture makers in New Mexico can work in the classic, stylistic languages of the Spanish or Mission styles, or international themes such as Classical or Art Deco.

A generation ago, such diversity did not exist in New Mexico and probably not in the western United States either. Today's impressive range of expression of Rio Grande high style is the result of an unprecedented migration of talent to the Southwest along with the renaissance of existing historical styles. The artists, designers, and craftsmen who embody the ideals of Rio Grande high style are creating a lasting legacy in American design.

Ray Fisher and his wife, Alice, migrated to New Mexico from New Jersey ten years ago and discovered a fresh range of expression for furniture art. Trained at the Newark School of Fine and Industrial Arts, Ray is a versatile artist who brings a freewheeling imagination to his work.

Fisher has produced an elegant ensemble of Art Deco-influenced furniture and light fixtures that, despite modern appearances, reflect a distinctive Southwestern pedigree. Ray adapted a detail from a Pueblo Deco building, the Southern Pacific Train Station in Casa Grande, Arizona, for the ornamentation on his Southwest Deco trastero. He has also developed a striking collection of light fixtures crafted of Corian, a new plastic with ethereally translucent qualities, introduced by Dupont.

Ray's design curiosity is restless, and he is always looking for a new departure. "After making something for ten or twenty times, I start looking around for something new to do. Right now, I'm thinking of making some new furniture based on the 1950s," Ray adds.

▲
Ray Fisher's
Southwestern Deco
armoire features a
parapet design
inspired by a
Pueblo Deco train
station in Arizona.
▼

BRUCE PETERSON
DIXON, NEW MEXICO

Near the small northern New Mexico village of Dixon, the banks of the Rio Grande nourish a surprising variety of trees, including juniper, cottonwood, willow, and tamarisk. Craftsman Bruce Peterson scavenges around here for special and select trees, which he cuts into planks and dries over a period of several years.

Peterson learned the secret of wood selection and handworking technique from the Swedish-born master James Krenov. By juxtaposing various hardwoods in patterns and carvings, Peterson achieves colorful and sublime effects in his furniture.

Bruce works in a style he has called Southwest Chippendale, and can be considered one of the innovators of a design attitude of fusion and manipulation of historical styles typical of postmodernism. In Peterson's hands, furniture expression is committed to the value of fine craftsmanship rather than pure style. Design influences from Chippendale or Frank Lloyd Wright remain subtle.

Peterson stays true to the Southwest, carving flora and fauna such as hummingbirds and yucca plants in his pieces. He remains one of a few artists employing a full palette of Rio Grande woods in his work.

▲

Bruce Peterson's "Southwest Chippendale" chair adopts the famous proportions and stance of the Chippendale style but is accented with Dixon willow-inlay panels.

▼

▲

A detail of Bruce Peterson's "Southwest Hummingbird" sideboard highlights his incredible woodcarving talents.

▼

Berkeley Mills
Studio of Santa Fe
has designed a
delicately tapered,
contemporary,
canopy bed.

An interior
designed by
Ray Fisher displays
a Southwestern Deco
bed, flanking
Moorish cabinets,
and light fixtures
crafted of
Corian plastic.

Arroyo Design's "Lorraine" chair employs the scrolled-arm motif common to the classical tradition of the Biedermeier style. The chair is made of cherry, and the small Biedermeier cabinet is shown in mesquite.

Andrew Davis celebrates a classical Corinthian column in his witty "Corinthian" jewelry box made of cherry and hollow tiger ash.

Christopher Thomson is a consummate craftsman—learning pottery from a Bauhaus-trained master, tuning his soul to the enigmatic pitch of flute music he studied in college, and ultimately becoming one of the Southwest's renowned ironworks artists.

With his wife, Susan Livermore, actively directing their company, Christopher's studio has grown to include five assistant ironworkers. The studio is located along the path of the Pecos River, just over thirty miles southeast of Santa Fe.

Downstream from the ruined Pecos pueblo, small Hispanic villages of San Miguel, San Jose, and Ribera nurture a host of artists, craftsmen, farmers, and wine makers, and this bucolic lifestyle surely inspires Thomson's work. His ironwork varies from expressionistic floor lamps (with entwined snakes) and candlesticks to the classical drama of his masterpiece, "Wave Bed."

Of his work, Christopher says, "I love the immediacy and freedom of forging hot metal. Though most of my designs are quite simple, I like to think that my life experiences and inspirations flow into my work and subtly encourage it to grow in personal directions. I feel extremely lucky to work in the windy shadow of Rowe Mesa with a crew of blacksmiths whose natural talents, energies, and ideas challenge and augment my own."

▲ **A** dramatic "Wave and Hearts" bed by Ribera, New Mexico, master craftsman Christopher Thomson articulates the traditional four-poster-bed form with vigorous dynamism. ▼

▲ **C**hristopher Thomson's dining chairs and table dramatically exploit the fluid qualities of wrought iron. ▼

JOHN SUTTMAN
ALBUQUERQUE, NEW MEXICO

Among the most architecturally minded of all Rio Grande furniture designers is John Suttman. Suttman trained as a sculptor and apprenticed in bronze-casting foundries in Rome and New Mexico.

Steel is John's medium of choice, and he has mastered its effects. Among his works are highly burnished, chrome-like tables and steel cabinets, patinaed to resemble wood. Besides his furniture art, Suttman produces architectural elements such as stairways and gates.

Style is an area where Suttman's work bridges the distinctions between modernism and postmodernism with a hearty dose of theatrical romanticism thrown in. Suttman loves the wavy rhythms and jazzy syncopation of the Art Deco style, employing it to great effect in table and banister designs. He is also comfortable with the rigid but soaring aspiration of the Gothic style, as seen in a surprising, recent cabinet. Above all, John Suttman's work is characterized by a cool precision that was an ideal of the Bauhaus masters.

▲ A steel, Gothic cabinet is nestled below an Art Deco-inspired staircase by John Suttman. ▼

▲ Welded-steel dining-room ensembles by John Suttman delight the eye with Art Deco cutout shapes. ▼

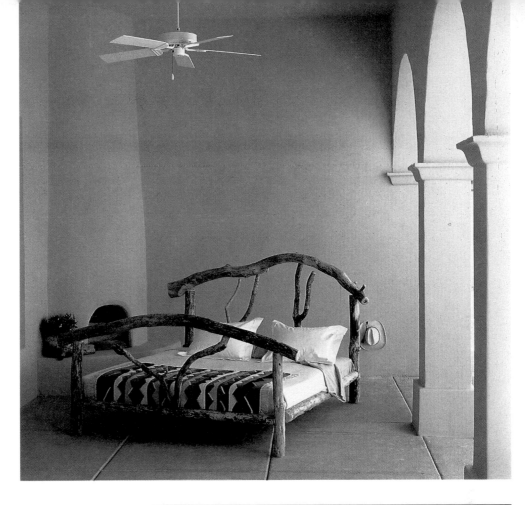

A rustic Ponderosa pine bed by Range Furniture adds a dramatic naturalistic counterpoint to a Mission-style setting.

ON NATURAL DESIGN. . . *"I got the idea for Range furniture from hiking in the forest. I began to notice all this rotting wood . . . and I began to see a potential hazard from it . . . from the insect infestation. So I was moved to try and make something from it . . . and that's how I came up with the idea for Range furniture.*

"I've always enjoyed these wonderful shapes. I'm not trying to contrive or control it. I'm trying to let the wood itself control the flow of the furniture. What's important to me is that each piece have its own movement.

"I'm amazed by Nature's own design. It's an art form."

MATT SCHUMACHER, RANGE STUDIO

Range Furniture of Flagstaff presents a sublime chest of drawers, crafted of recycled forest wood. The cabinet breathes a Zen-like quality of tranquil balance. The design is animated by the random imperfection of the rustic twig handles, which appear to float above the piece.

ROD HOUSTON
ILFELD, NEW MEXICO

Rod Houston has lived near Santa Fe for nearly twenty years and is still in awe of the New Mexican landscape. In Rod's words, "Living in the Southwest, I find myself constantly seeking a personal style that expresses my reverence for this unique landscape. The naked rock, jagged canyons, and snaking rivers have made devotees of many (newcomers) . . .; my pieces are, in a sense, a journal of my experiences. A sheet of ice forming a bridge from riverbank to midstream suggests a table. Many designs begin as fleeting thoughts or chance visual encounters. . . . Among my recent work are pieces first envisioned years ago."

Rod graduated from the University of Southern California with a degree in geology, and first approached furniture design with a Japanese taste for simplicity. His style evolved gradually to include some minimal ornamentation, including Pueblo and Classical motifs; but structure and form are paramount for Houston.

Rod Houston's foyer table is a neo-classical innovation, inspired by the light and refined classicism of the colonial Hepplewhite style, popular about 1800. A Greek wave motif graces the table and mirror.

"Roadside Geology" is the name of Rod Houston's inventive, upright cabinet. Inspired by the artist's love of geology, the cabinet features a variety of luxury hardwoods including walnut, lacewood, ash, and mahogany.

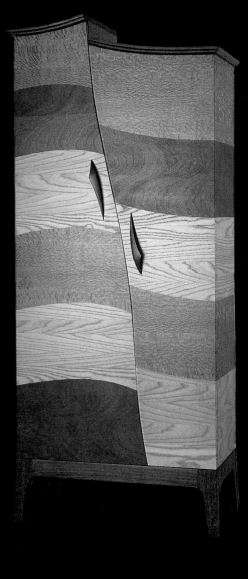

A carved, strap-work rocking chair by Peter Gould of Santa Fe boldly expresses contemporary Rio Grande design. Chip-carved accents evoke the Spanish Colonial tradition, but otherwise the chair is a progressive example of contemporary Santa Fe furniture. The chair stands in front of a painted willow screen by Sombrajé.

In his elegant sideboard crafted of Honduras mahogany, John Sheriff borrows from the refined classical style of the Hepplewhite tradition, popular in the eastern American states after the Revolution.

ACCESSORIES

Near the New Mexico and Colorado border, where the Rio Grande cuts a swath through wildly beautiful and verdant jagged mountains, lush meadows lie that have nurtured livestock and people for over two centuries. The earth itself is painted dramatically, and the picturesque adobe village of Tierra Amarilla is named for the yellow clay deposits in the area.

Scottsdale, Arizona's, Que Pasa design store offers many exciting Rio Grande furnishings and accessories, including Indian dolls, equipale dinette set and love seat, a faux-finish armoire, and an overstuffed chair with hand-painted upholstery.

One hundred and twenty-five years ago, gigantic flocks of sheep roamed this country, providing wool and mutton for export to far-off cities in Mexico and California. By 1970, the great flocks vanished, and the Rio Arriba (upper river) country desperately sought other sources of revenue.

A determined group of ranchers and their families organized into an agricultural and weaving cooperative called Ganados del Valle, headquartered in Los Ojos, New Mexico, and began the long process of reintroducing the traditional lifestyle of sheep ranching and weaving into northern New Mexico. The group concentrated its efforts on raising *churro* sheep, a hardy Spanish breed known for its lustrous, long fleeces—the source of authentic, Rio Grande weaving quality.

Today, Ganados del Valle is a thriving rural cooperative, honored and recognized nationally for its remarkable efforts to train people in the lost arts of sheep industry and Rio Grande weaving. Artisans weave many products, including blankets, rugs, and clothing in the gorgeous Rio Grande style, both in traditional and contemporary patterns.

Santa Fe Lights offers ceramic light fixtures with a modern, streamlined appearance.

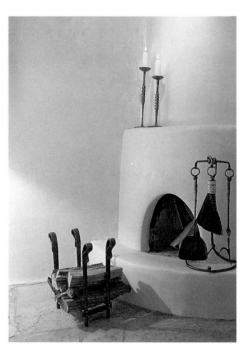

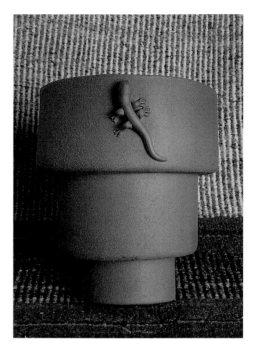

An adobe kiva fireplace is a natural setting for a fireplace set and a candlestick holder by Christopher Thomson Ironworks of Ribera, New Mexico.

Robin Reindle lives in the small village of Terrero, New Mexico, and crafts exceptional, ceramic wall sconces in a Rio Grande style.

Rio Grande furniture has provided the focal point of an integrated, interior-design style unique to the American Southwest for over three centuries. Interiors of early New Mexican homes were crude and sparse by modern standards but still possessed a distinctive charm.

RIO GRANDE INTERIORS

The massive trasteros and cajas with locks were the prized possessions on the frontier. A small table and perhaps one or two chairs were the pride of a prosperous family. Otherwise, seating was provided on a built-in adobe banco, or most people just sat on the floor on hides. Beds were unknown in Spanish Colonial New Mexico. Rough mattresses were crafted of sheared wool and heavy cloth. Buffalo and other hides could also be used as bedding.

The other necessities of life were painstakingly handcrafted but lovingly adorned. Both men and women wove blankets in a distinctive style now known as Rio Grande style. Rio Grande-style weaving was developed to a high degree in northern New Mexico villages near sheep-raising centers in the high mountains north of Santa Fe. Villages such as Tierra Amarilla, Abiquiu, Chimayo, and Cordova developed significant weaving traditions that are still flourishing today.

Both Rio Grande and Navajo weaving reached high levels of technical excellence and artistry in the nineteenth century. Rio Grande weaving patterns were highly influenced by the central-diamond motif, which dominated popular imported Mexican shawls (called the Saltillo style), and central diamonds also appear on Navajo blankets after 1850. Otherwise, Rio Grande-style weavings are simple and elegant, featuring stripes, diamonds, and thunderbird designs.

During the Spanish Colonial era, religious folk art was practiced out of devotion and necessity. The long and hazardous overland trading route between Mexico City and Santa Fe, called El Camino Real (The Royal Road), prevented large and fragile objects, especially delicate religious statues and paintings, from being transported to the northern frontier.

Instructed by friars, artists in New Mexico learned to fashion their own religious figures out of wood and natural pigments. Most popular art forms include the *bultos* (statues in the round) and *retablos* (flat wall plaques). Very limited tools and other basic necessities such as glue and sandpaper restricted the finishes and expression of the folk art. Authentic religious folk art of New Mexico appears crude and naive but is endowed with powerful emotion. Modern santeros have produced highly finished and lustrous works but still strive to capture the essence of religious devotion that distinguishes Rio Grande art. Many designers and homemakers consider New Mexican religious art an essential component of the Rio Grande-style interior.

After the opening of the Southwestern frontier with the Santa Fe Trail in 1821 and the Mexican War in 1848, new products for the home drastically changed New Mexican lifestyles.

Common materials such as glass, milled lumber, nails, textiles, lamps, and other necessities were highly sought after imported goods. Still, many of these luxuries did not reach isolated mountain villages for many years. New Mexicans learned to imitate or replicate household goods with available resources. The art of tinwork, developed in the nineteenth century after tin cans were imported from the United States by the U.S. Army and other American pioneers, was developed into a sophisticated and beautiful craft.

A lovely, tapered, Pueblo Deco mirror by Albuquerque designer Marc Coan captures a spirit of contemporary Rio Grande style.

Marc Coan's jewelry boxes represent his most recent work. In a postmodern, Pueblo Deco style, the boxes combine painted and natural woods and vinyl-composition tile accents.

Among the most popular tinwork products in the nineteenth century were picture frames, candelabras, sconces, and crosses. During the Spanish Colonial Revival of the 1930s, tinwork was adapted to many more practical household uses. Exquisite tin mailboxes, tissue holders, Christmas ornaments, wastebaskets, platters, mirrors, and electric light fixtures were sold at the Native Market in Santa Fe along with the traditional tin products.

During the 1950s, when suburbanization and mass production homogenized American society, the demand for unique folk art products waned, and New Mexican tin craft declined. By 1970, only a few families, significantly the Sandovals of Albuquerque and the Delgados of Santa Fe, continued the tradition. With the resurgence of Rio Grande style, tinwork is also being revived. Young tinsmiths are producing high quality works with new inventiveness. Tin is being rediscovered and manipulated by artists as a new material, and new household applications are appearing, such as kitchen cabinet doors and refrigerator ornamentation.

Wrought-iron work has ancient roots in the Hispanic way of life, and the blacksmith was an essential member of any frontier expedition or colonization. Often the blacksmith assisted the carpenter in producing furniture by crafting hardware such as hinges and locks. Today, ironwork is a vital component of the Rio Grande style.

Wrought-iron studios are flourishing in New Mexico, satisfying a surging demand for authentic door and furniture hardware, light fixtures, fireplace accessories, curtain rods, and other home products. Recently, blacksmiths

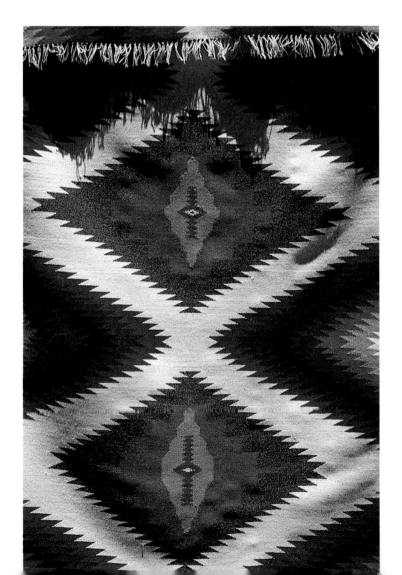

Rio Grande Spanish weaving tradition is characterized by the use of traditional natural dyes and design patterns. Shown here is a double Saltillo-diamond design derived from the Mexican tapestry design that was popular in New Mexico in the nineteenth century.

The tradition of painted and inlaid tiles can be easily traced to Morocco. Painted-tile designs are welcome in any Rio Grande home.

Religious folk art, known in New Mexico as santos, makes a colorful and attractive accessory for Rio Grande furniture.

have expanded their art to include furniture ensembles. The most dramatic Rio Grande iron accessories include elaborate canopy and four-poster beds, patio furniture, coffee and sofa tables, and lamps.

The Rio Grande region is known throughout the world for its superb Native American ceramics, and so it is natural that extraordinary ceramic accessories are available for home use and decoration. Unlimited styles and sizes of tiles are available for floors, bathrooms, and kitchens. Colorful ceramics from Mexico, Latin America, and Spain are sold in New Mexico to offer the designer an extraordinary palette of effects. Ceramic sconces and lighting fixtures are among the most innovative clay product for Rio Grande high style.

With a dazzling array of furniture and accessories currently available, very few regions of the United States or the world can match the dynamic creativity of the Rio Grande style. Only the imagination of the designer can limit the effects and moods possible in its spectrum.

Jim Wagner of Taos, New Mexico, crafts exceptional ceramic wall sconces in a Rio Grande style.

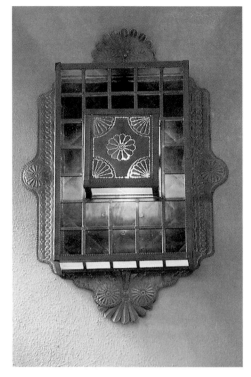

The Spanish Colonial rosette design becomes an effective candle wall sconce crafted by J. D. Martinez of Española.

Painted glass and tinwork combine to great effect in this Santa Fe electric light sconce.

Dimestore Cowboys of Albuquerque offers an interesting variety of hand-forged hardware and accessories for Rio Grande homes.

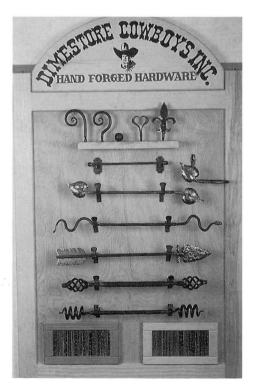

John Bauer's
"Six Rabbit" mirror
is a pleasing
excercise utilizing
light and dark woods
to achieve an
illusion of movement.

A Pueblo thunder-
bird becomes a
stylized, Pueblo
Deco-style lighting
sconce in Santa Fe.

R E S O U R C E S

NEW SPANISH STYLE

Artisans of the Desert
1625 Fourth Street NW
Albuquerque, NM 87102
(800) 827-9725
Maker: Chris Sandoval/
Mark Carrico

Blue Canyon Woodwork
1310 Siler Road #1
Santa Fe, NM 87501
(505) 471-0136
Maker: Larry Hulsey/Staff

Blue Sky Woodworks
P.O. Box 255
Corrales, NM 87504
(505) 473-0464

Dell Woodworks
1326 Rufina Circle
Santa Fe, NM 87501
(505) 471-6336
Maker: John Dell/Staff

Ernest Thompson Furniture
2618 Coors Road SW
Albuquerque, NM 87121
(505) 873-4652
Maker: Mike and Doreen
Godwin/Staff

Esperanza Fine Furniture
P.O. Box 374
Albuquerque, NM 87103
(505) 898-2597

Gallegos
Route 9, Box 81A
Santa Fe, NM 87505
(505) 983-1313
Maker: Roberto Gallegos

Greg Flores Furniture
120 Bent Street,
P.O. Box 2
Taos, NM 87571
(505) 758-8010
Maker: Greg Flores

Luis Tapia
C/O Owings/Dewey
    Fine Art
74 East San Francisco
Santa Fe, NM 87501
(505) 982-6244
Maker: Luis Tapia

McMillan's Old Santa Fe
Furniture Co.
6600 Cerrillos Road
Santa Fe, NM 87501
(505) 471-4934

Prudencio Woodworks
6507 Christy NE
Albuquerque, NM 87109
(505) 344-9225
Maker: Frederico Prudencio

Rio Viento Woodworking
Santa Fe, NM 87501
(505) 471-5169
Maker: Philip Alarid

Sangre de Cristo
    Woodworkers
P.O. Box 125
Costilla, NM 87524
(505) 586-1102

Santa Fe Country Furniture
1708 Cerrillos Road
Santa Fe, NM 87505
(505) 984-1478

Santa Fe Doors
P.O. Box 6322
Albuquerque, NM 87197
(505) 345-3160

Santa Fe Heritage
530 Montezuma-
Sanbusco Center
Santa Fe, NM 87501
(505) 983-5986
Maker: Larry DeLeon/Staff

Southwest Spanish Craftsmen
328 South Guadalupe
Santa Fe, NM 87504
(505) 982-1767
Maker: Roger Nussbaumer/
    Staff

Spanish Pueblo Doors
P.O. Box 2517;
1091-B Siler Road
Santa Fe, NM 87504
(505) 473-0464

Studio, Abad Lucero
1017 Aztec NW
Santa Fe, NM 87107
Phone: unknown
Maker: Abad Lucero

Studio, George P. Sandoval
3718 Second Street NW
Albuquerque, NM 87107
(505) 345-9442
    or 344-6021
Maker: George P. Sandoval

Studio, Michael Trujillo
H CR 74, Box 22315
El Prado, NM 87529
(505) 751-1401
Maker: Michael Trujillo

Studio, David E. C'de Baca
Route 14, Box 234D
Santa Fe, NM 87506
Phone: unknown
Maker: David E. C'deBaca

Studio, William Cabrera
312 1/2 North 3rd Street
Grants, NM 87020
(505) 287-3929
Maker: William Cabrera

Studio, Ramon Jose Lopez
P.O. Box 2495
Santa Fe, NM 87504-2495
(505) 988-4976
Maker: Ramon Jose Lopez

Studio, Raymond Lopez
Route 11, Box 21011
Santa Fe, NM 87501
Phone: unknown
Maker: Raymond Lopez

Studio, Anthony Martinez
Address: P.O. Box 305
Española, NM 87532
(505) 753-3558
Maker: Anthony Martinez

Studio, Paul Martinez
P.O. Box 1516
Ranchos de Taos, NM 87557
(505) 751-0475
Maker: Paul Martinez

Studio, Lawrence Quintana
1224 Gallegos Lane
Santa Fe, NM 87501
Phone: unknown
Maker: Lawrence Quintana

Studio, Fred Romero
P.O. Box 155
Santa Cruz, NM 87567-
   0155
Phone: unknown
Maker: Fred Romero

Studio, Tim Roybal
P.O. Box 1726
Española, NM 87532
Phone: unknown
Maker: Tim Roybal

Taos Furniture
P.O. Box 5555, Dept. DK,
   1807 Second Street
Santa Fe, NM 87502
(505) 988-1229 or
   800-443-3448

Taos Wood Design
P.O. Box 1125
Taos, NM 87571
(505) 758-9060
Maker: Mark Romero

Worrlein Studio
11 La Junta Road
Lamy, NM 87540
(505) 466-7777
Maker: Gunther Worrlein

TAOS COUNTRY STYLE

Brenden & Company
P.O. Box 175
Dixon, NM 87527
(505) 579-4696
Maker: Robert Brenden

Country Furnishings of Taos
P.O. Box 2047
534 North Pueblo Road
Taos, NM 87541
(505) 758-4633
Maker: Mary Shriver/Staff

Land of the Wildgoose
Dixon, NM 87527
(505) 579-4447
Maker: Michael Wildgoose

Mark Manville
P.O. Box 1234
Ranchos de Taos, NM 87557
(505) 758-5565
Maker: Mark Manville

Sombrajé Collection
544 South Guadalupe
Santa Fe, NM 87501
(505) 988-5567
Maker: Hillary Riggs

Southwest Adirondack
P.O. Box 86
Rinconada, NM 87531
(505) 579-4499
Maker: Jake Harwell

Jim Wagner
C/O The Parks Gallery
106 Dona Luz
Taos, NM 87571
(505) 751-0343
Maker: Jim Wagner

Woolam Studios
P.O. Box 246
Arroyo Seco, NM 87514
(505) 776-1851
Maker: Chris Woolam

MISSION/CRAFTSMEN

Arroyo Design
24 No. 4th Avenue
Tuson, AZ 85705
(602) 884-1012
Makers: Stephen and
   Elaine Paul

Berkeley Mills Furniture
   Company
1714 Paseo de Peralta
Santa Fe, NM 87501
(505) 982-4584
Maker: Dave Kent/Staff

Chamiza Prairie
100 Alameda Road NW
Albuquerque, NM 87114
(505) 897-1365
Maker: Anna Patalano

Chapparal Studios
 P.O. Box 22249
Santa Fe, NM 87502
(800) 428-0612
Maker: Stephen Pino/Staff

Country Primitives
2887 Industrial Road
Santa Fe, NM 87501
(505) 984-8271

Creations in Wood
1370 East 8th Street, Ste 4
Tempe, AZ 85381
(602) 929-0132

Randolph Laub Studio
310 Johnson Street
Santa Fe, NM 87501
(505) 984-0081
Maker: Randolph Laub

COWBOY AND
RANCH STYLE

The Cowboy Collection
9255 Doheny Road #3004
Los Angeles, CA 90069
(310) 550-8342
Maker: Lenore Mulligan/Staff

Cowboy Classics
364 Main Street
Longmont, CO 80501
(303) 776-3394
Maker: Tom and Maril Bice

Due West Furniture
Box 2758
Rindge, NH 03461
(603) 899-5259
Maker: Elizabeth Howe/Staff

Into the West
P.O. Box 880767
Steamboat Springs, CO
   80488
(303) 879-8377
Maker: Jace Romick

L. D. Burke Furniture
1516 Pacheco Street
Santa Fe, NM 87501
(505) 986-1866
Maker: L. D. Burke

Livingston Furniture Design
P.O. Box 2022
Hutchinson, KS 67504
(316) 662-2781
Maker: Mike Livingston

The Naturalist
1080 South 350 East
Provo, UT 84606
(800) 344-7244

Nellie Barr Furniture
3652 North Tripp Avenue
Chicago, IL 60641
(312) 202-1970
Maker: Cathryn Slaga

Rockin' Moon Enterprises
P.O. Box 70
Ft. Lupton, CO 80621
(303) 857-4181
Maker: Frank Hobbs

Rustic Ranch Furnishings
P.O. Box 1237
Terrell, TX 75160
(214) 524-8894

Milo Marks
Box 208, Highway 6
Meridian, TX 76665
(817) 435-2173
Maker: Milo Marks

Wild West Woodworks
P.O. Box 448
Eagar, AZ 85925
(602) 333-4548
Maker: Bill Greenwood

Woodwright
#3 Raven Ridge Road
Lamy, NM 87540
(505) 982-1549
Makers: Robin, Connie and
   Ryan Doughman

ACCESSORIES

Adobe Elegance
Department SP
Route 3, Box 37
Terrero, NM 87573
(505) 757-2518

Architectural Ironworks
433 West San Francisco
Santa Fe, NM 87501
(505) 989-1059

The Chile Shop
109 East Water Street
Santa Fe, NM 87501
(505) 983-6080

Christopher Thomson
P.O. Box 578
Ribera, NM 87560
(505) 421-2645
Maker: Christopher Thomson

Coan Woodworks
3090 Arenal SW
Albuquerque, NM 87105
(505) 877-5707
Maker: Marc Coan

Form + Function
328 South Guadalupe
Santa Fe, NM 87501
(505) 455-2864

Franzetti Design
P.O. Box 997
Rancho de Taos, NM 87557
(505) 758-8471

Galeria San Isidro, Inc.
P.O. Box 17913
El Paso, TX 79917-7913
(915) 858-5222
Maker: Harl Dixon

Galisteo
590 Tenth Street
San Francisco, CA 94103
(415) 861-5900

G-T Stained Glass & Tinworks
1433 Central Avenue NW
Albuquerque, NM 87104
(505) 247-9322
Maker: Ted and Ginny
     Arellanes

DiMatteo Interiors
P.O. Box 9034
Santa Fe, NM 87504
(505) 982-4784
Furniture Specialty:
     Interior Design

Dimestore Cowboys
4500 Hawkins NE
Albuquerque, NM 87109
(505) 345-3933
Furniture Specialty: Hardware

Hasty's & Kram's
4716 Second Street NW
Albuquerque, NM 87107
(505) 343-1751

La Mesa of Santa Fe
225 Canyon Road
Santa Fe, NM 87501
(505) 984-1688

Lo Fino
P.O. Box 6345,
201 Paseo
Taos, NM 87571
(505) 758-0298
(Furniture also available)

Mah-Lin-Dah's
29 West Water Street
Santa Fe, NM 87501
(505) 983-2778

Paseo Pottery
1424 Paseo de Peralta
Santa Fe, NM 87501
(505) 988-7687

Raul Zea Ironwork
325 Homesite Lane NW
Albuquerque, NM 87114
(505) 897-0577
Maker: Raul Zea

Sandoval Studio
7222 Vivian NE
Albuquerque, NM 87109
(505) 821-4476
Maker: Bonifacio Sandoval
Furniture Specialty: Tinwork

Santa Fe
3571 Sacramento Street
San Francisco, CA 94118
(415) 346-0180

Santa Fe Interiors
214 Old Santa Fe Trail
Santa Fe, NM 87501
(505) 988-2227

Santa Fe Lights
Dept. N, Route 10, Box 88-Y
Santa Fe, NM 87501
(505) 471-0076

Santa Fe Lightscapes
2918 Rufina Court
Santa Fe, NM 87501
(505) 438-8896

Santa Fe Tinworks
P.O. Box 1002
Santa Fe, NM 87504-1002
(505) 983-1275

Schlien Quilts
201 Galisteo Street
Santa Fe, NM 87501
(505) 983-7370
Maker: Lily/Wolf Schlien

Seret & Sons
149 East Alameda
Santa Fe, NM 87501
(505) 988-9151
Furniture Specialty: Kilims

Streck Family
541 West Cordova Road
Santa Fe, NM 87501
(505) 986-1201

Strictly Southwestern
1321 Eubank NE
Albuquerque, NM 87112
(505) 292-7337

Studio, William Cabrera
312 1/2 North 3rd Street
Grants, NM 87020
(505) 287-3929
Maker: William Cabrera

Sun Dagger Design
P.O. Box 4355
Santa Fe, NM 87502
(505) 455-2864

Tecolote Tiles & Gallery
400 San Felipe NW
Old Town
Albuquerque, NM 87104
(505) 243-3403

West by Southwest
110 West Quince
Farmington, NM 87401
(800) 582-5688
Maker: Guylyn Durham/Staff

Yippie-ei-o!
7051 Fifth Avenue
Scottsdale, AZ 85251
(800) 841-5947

NATIVE AMERICAN

Elizabeth Drey Collection
209 Galisteo
Santa Fe, NM 87501
(505) 989-7719
Maker: Elizabeth Drey/Staff

John L. Bauer Furniture
Route 19, Box 89-TM
Santa Fe, NM 87505
(505) 982-4399
Maker: John L. Bauer

Sovereign Native
16010 West 5th Avenue, # 8
Golden, CO 80401
(303) 278-8099
Maker: Douglas Rich

The Old West Collection
P.O. Box 4611
Aspen, CO 81612
(303) 925-4799
Maker: Cassandra Lohr/Staff

West by Southwest
110 West Quince
Farmington, NM 87401
(800) 582-5688
Maker: Guylyn Durham/Staff

Zuni Furniture Enterprise
P.O. Box 339
Zuni, NM 87327
(505) 782-5855

SOUTHWEST CONTEMPORARY

Adobe Accents
7601 East Gray Road
Scottsdale, AZ 85260
(505) 991-2638

Furniture of Santa Fe-
Olea, Inc.
101 West Marcy
Santa Fe, NM 87501
(505) 985-1895

Linson's Manufacturing
Route 16, Box 198JJ
Santa Fe, NM 87505
(505) 473-2855
Maker: Chris Linson

Palo Duro Woodworking
2897 Trades West Road
Santa Fe, NM 87501
(505) 471-3637

Santa Fe Trade
Route 5, Box 215
Santa Fe, NM 87501
(505) 455-7455

CONTEMPORARY CRAFTSMEN STYLE

Adam Eisman Woodworking
425 Camino Monte Vista
Santa Fe, NM 87501
(303) 989-8994
Maker: Adam Eisman

Adobe Furniture
1319 Conant
Dallas, TX 75207
(214) 637-3989
Maker: Butch Hale

Arroyo Design
224 North 4th Avenue
Tucson, AZ 85705
(602) 884-1012

Arizona Range Furniture
2423 North Cypress Point
Flagstaff, AZ 86004
(602) 527-4179
Maker: Matt Schumacher

Charles & David Interiors
205 Delgado Street
Santa Fe, NM 87501
(505) 988-9629
Maker: Gene Law

Christopher Thomson
P.O. Box 578
Ribera, NM 87560
(505) 421-2645
Maker: Christopher Thomson,

Coan Woodworks
3090 Arenal SW
Albuquerque, NM 87105
(505) 877-5707
Maker: Marc Coan

Cottonwood Images
P.O. Box 1006
Taos, NM 87571
(505)758-1726
Maker: Benjamin Carp

Doolings of Santa Fe
525 Airport Road
Santa Fe, NM 87501
(505) 471-5956
Maker: Rob Dooling/Staff

Galeria San Isidro, Inc.
P.O. Box 17913
El Paso, TX 79917-7913
(915) 858-5222
Maker: Harl Dixon

Peter Gould
544 South Guadalupe
Santa Fe, NM 87501
(505) 984-3045
Maker: Peter Gould

Gowen's
1919 Old Town Road,
Suite 3
Albuquerque, NM 87104
(505) 842-9089
Maker: Greg Gowen

J & C Custom Metalwork
1550 B. Pacheco Street #5
Santa Fe, NM 87501
(505) 989-1747

Kent Galleries
130 Lincoln Avenue
Santa Fe, NM 87501
(505) 988-1001
Makers: Rod Houston, John
Sheriff, Bruce Peterson,
John Suttman, Andrew
Davis, Larry and Nancy
Buechley, and Mike Bartell

John R. Keyser
160 West Meadowlark
Corrales, NM 87048
(505) 897-0468
Maker: John R. Keyser

Kozlowski Woodworks
P.O. Box 8316
Santa Fe, NM 87504
(505) 989-9189
Maker: David Kozlowski

Lloyd Kreitz Studio
1808 Second Street A
Santa Fe, NM 87505
(505) 984-1841
Maker: Lloyd Kreitz

Mesilla Woodworks
2011 Avenida de Mesilla
Las Cruces, NM 88005
(505) 523-1362
Maker: Neal McMillan

Morelli Furniture
701 Alarid Street
Santa Fe, NM 87501
(505) 984-1587
Maker: Jeremy Morelli

Raul Zea Ironwork
325 Homesite Lane NW
Albuquerque, NM 87114
(505) 897-0577
Maker: Raul Zea

Ray Fisher Designs
3 Amistad Place
Santa Fe, NM 87505
(505) 466-8949
Maker: Ray Fisher

Rod Houston Woodwork
Rural Route Station
Ilfeld, NM 87538
(505) 421-2744
Maker: Rod Houston

Seckler Studio
150 South St. Francis Drive
Santa Fe, NM 87501
(505) 989-4370
Maker: Frank Seckler

Southwest Stoneworks
P.O. Box 248
Dixon, NM 87527
(505) 689-2333
Maker: Mark Saxe

Streck Family
541 West Cordova Road
Santa Fe, NM 87501
(505) 986-1201

Worrlein Studio
11 La Junta Road
Lamy, NM 87540
(505) 466-7777
Maker: Gunther Worrlein

WWW Designs
P.O. Box 1058
Ranchos de Taos, NM 87557
(505) 758-0477
Maker: Wendy Wysong

USEFUL WORDS—
GLOSSARY OF TERMS

Adze: a hatchet-like tool with a flat blade head, commonly used in Spanish Colonial furniture to plane wood, leaving a distinctive, rough-textured surface.

Armoire: a French word for a cabinet used to store armor. In American furniture, an armoire is a great, upright chest with two panel doors, used to store clothing; a wardrobe. The common Spanish word for an armoire is *ropero*.

Baroque: a style of decoration and also a historic period of architecture and interior design that followed the Renaissance in the sixteenth and seventeenth centuries. Baroque describes a highly ornamented, often gilded fashion utilizing rich materials such as fine hardwoods and marble. Baroque is the opposite of plain and simple.

Caja: a Spanish word meaning "box." More accurately, it describes a chest in the Spanish Colonial tradition. Spanish chests can be made with or without legs and commonly feature elaborate locks. Chests may be carved and were often painted. Many Spanish chests feature carving inspired by Moorish examples (*see* Moorish).

Chimayó: an old Native American and Hispanic settlement located twenty-five miles north of Santa Fe, New Mexico. Chimayó has fostered a rich tradition of Rio Grande weaving, which has been used to upholster western furniture.

Chip-carving: the technique employed to carve designs into Spanish Colonial furniture. Using a hammer and a variety of chisels, the craftsman outlines designs in pencil and then gouges out chips of wood to achieve a beautiful, bas-relief effect.

Chippendale: a style of furniture made famous by English cabinetmaker Thomas Chippendale (1718-79). Highly influential in the American colonies, Chippendale furniture became the rage on the Eastern seaboard after 1755. Chippendale furniture is characterized by classical details, elaborate carving, and pedimented cabinets. Chippendale is also a classic American style that is influential in furniture and architecture such as Phillip Johnson's AT & T Tower in Manhattan, even appearing in some Southwestern pieces.

Colonial: the Spanish Colonial period in the Southwest, which lasted from 1540, when Francisco Vasquez de Coronado first explored the region, to 1821, when Mexico won her independence from Spain. Mexico ruled the Southwest until 1848, when the United States won the Mexican War and gained the Southwest in the Treaty of Guadalupe Hidalgo.

Colter, Mary: the staff architect for the Santa Fe Railroad during the early twentieth century, who often collaborated with Fred Harvey on his "Harvey houses." She had an inspired sense of Southwest style, furnishing the hotels with an eclectic mix of Mission, wicker, buckskin, and other classic themes.

Concha: a Spanish word meaning "shell." It also refers to a shell-like ornament, usually silver, which is a common feature of Indian jewelry but may also be applied to furniture. Some contemporary Southwestern designers are attaching silver, tin, or copper conchas to their cabinets and tables.

Distressing: a finishing technique that became popular in the 1980s, probably influenced by Hollywood designers who wanted to create an instant finish effect of great age or antiquity. Wood may be stained, scratched, sandblasted, beaten with chains, or any other inventive technique designed to "distress" the wood surface and make it appear old.

Eastlake: a style and theory of furniture and home furnishings made popular by Charles Locke

Eastlake, an English writer after 1868. Eastlake's ideas influenced the American Arts and Crafts movement and the nearly identical Mission style, emphasizing simplification and less ornamentation than the sometimes frivolous Victorian styles of his era.

Empire: a classical style derived from the interpretation of Greek furniture that was in high fashion about 1800. It later influenced some New Mexican furniture.

Fechin, Nicolai: a great Russian artist who lived in Taos, New Mexico, from 1927 to 1933. He fused Russian and Spanish Colonial furniture techniques, creating an original expression that is still being reproduced today.

Greek Revival: a style popular in the Southwest after it was introduced by the U. S. Army at forts in New Mexico after 1850 (see Territorial).

Greene and Greene: perhaps the most famous brothers in American architecture. Charles Sumner Greene and Henry Mather Greene practiced architecture and furniture design in California from approximately 1900 to 1930. They raised bungalow architecture and Craftsmen furniture to a high art, often

using sophisticated, Japanese joinery techniques. Greene and Greene still influence Southwestern Mission-style furniture.

Hardware: refers to locks, hinges, drawer pulls, and other functional metal parts of furniture. Often wrought iron, Southwestern hardware has become a delightful detail of furniture design, incorporating surprising materials and effects such as bone, tin, or copper.

Harvey, Fred: the legendary hotelier of the Santa Fe Railroad who created romantic oases of great architecture (often Mission style) in hotels across the Southwest in the early decades of the twentieth century. "Harvey houses" also provided early examples of impeccable interior design in the Southwestern style.

Joinery: the art and technique of joining two pieces (or more) of wood together. Some common wood joints are mortise-and-tenon, dovetail, rabbet, and dado.

Mesa: a Spanish word meaning "table." Spanish Colonial tables were often small, due to the lack of quality tools on the New Mexican frontier and the enormous effort required to fashion planks.

Missions: a colonization strategy employed by the Spanish that centered on a church, dormitories, stables, gardens, and other necessities of survival on the frontier. New Mexico, Arizona, Texas, and California have preserved mission complexes. The California Mission style was revived after 1890 and swept the West in popularity until about 1930. Arts and Crafts furniture of this era was also known as Craftsmen or Mission.

Molesworth, Thomas: the legendary, Cowboy-style designer from Cody, Wyoming. He fashioned inventive western furniture out of burled fir, leather, antlers, and other unusual materials from the 1930s to the 1970s. Recently, Molesworth's style of furniture has been revived by a colony of furniture designers in the northern Rockies, mostly from Colorado, Wyoming, and Montana.

Moorish: carving designs that influenced Spanish Colonial furniture in New Mexico.

Morris chair: the classic piece of Craftsmen- or Mission-style furniture. The Morris chair features generous proportions, an inclined back, oak and leather materials, and a simple, refined design.

Mortise-and-tenon: a type of wood joint commonly used in New Mexican and Hispanic furniture. One end of a wooden element is shaped into a male rectangular peg (tenon) designed to fit into a square socket (mortise). The tenon ends may be concealed, exposed, or extended beyond the joint frame, which is a common decorative element in Mission furniture. The joint is commonly pegged for stability.

Mudejar: the distinctive Spanish style that was created by using a blend of Moorish and European influences. Mudejar furniture features rich carving, the use of wrought-iron bracing and hardware, and classic European forms such as Italian Renaissance and Gothic.

Panels: the surfaces on cabinet doors that offer the craftsman an opportunity for self-expression. In Southwestern furniture, panels may be carved, inset with punched-tin designs, painted, or built up with applied moldings.

Pendleton: Pendleton Mills of Oregon has produced popular woolen blankets for over a century. Pendleton blankets in western and Native American designs are being used today as attractive upholstery fabric.

Pie safe: a traditional American Country-style cabinet featuring punched-tin panels for ventilations. Similar to the Spanish Colonial trastero, the pie-safe has influenced some New Mexican, upright cabinet designs.

Priest's chair: the classic New Mexican armchair. Patterned after medieval European throne designs, the priest's chair was a rare luxury on the southwestern frontier, reserved for a person of stature, such as the village priest or the master of the household. The considerable labor required to craft the armchair explains its great value and timeless appeal.

Proportions: have changed noticeably through the centuries of Southwestern design. Rare examples of early eighteenth-century, New Mexican Spanish Colonial furniture are small and crude, due to the difficulty of making long boards. Furniture proportions expanded with the Yankee influence after 1850, and contemporary dimensions have been tailored to meet modern uses, such as accommodating projection televisions and large sofas.

Rosette: a carved floral motif common in Spanish Colonial-furniture design. Rosettes are often circular, featuring scallop-carved petals. The rosette's origin is based on the Moorish style, along with carved lions, crosses, or interwoven border designs.

Settee: a form of bench or sofa seating. In the Craftsmen style, it's also known as a "settle." Settees ranged in size from intimate, two-person benches to the large lounges that became "Taos beds" when adapted by New Mexican furniture makers. Settees often feature a seat cushion.

Shaker: a refined, minimalist furniture style that has influenced some contemporary Southwestern furniture design. Shaker style was developed by the Shaker religious community of Pennsylvania, which values functional design and restrained ornamentation.

Silla: a Spanish word meaning "chair." Silla refers to an armless or side chair, and *sillon* describes an armchair of larger proportions, such as a priest's chair.

Stickley: the most famous name in American Arts and Crafts furniture. Gustav and his brothers, Leopold and J. G., developed furniture companies that crafted simple, durable Craftsmen furniture of solid oak and leather. Stickley furniture is among the most collectible of twentieth-century furniture.

Taos bed: a distinctive large sofa or lounge with a deep seat, wide enough to accommodate a sleeping person, hence the name. Derived from Craftsmen settees, the Taos bed made its appearance in New Mexico at the turn of the century.

Territorial: a hybrid style of Spanish Colonial and American mix that was developed in the Southwest after 1820. In California, the Territorial style featured strong New England influence from the Boston-based shipping companies. In New Mexico, the Territorial style acquired a classical, Greek Revival appearance from the U.S. Army forts. Later, Territorial-style furniture in New Mexico was transformed by Victorian styles.

Trastero: a large upright cabinet, such as a cupboard. In New Mexico, the trastero is the signature furniture piece, often displaying the carpenter's skills of joinery, carving, and finishing.

Wagner, Jim: a well-known Taos artist who pioneered Taos Country style in the 1980s. His painted cabinets and furniture celebrate common New Mexican animals such as dogs, magpies, rabbits, and trout; are finished in bold, lyrical colors; and are often drawn with a sense of humor.

Wright, Frank Lloyd: is generally considered the dean of modern American architecture. His early furniture designs were influenced by Arts and Crafts and early modernist ideals, and they still influence some of today's Rio Grande designers.

PHOTOGRAPHIC CREDITS

Ahlborn, Richard; p. 13
Davis, Wyatt; p. 14
Fuller, Tim; p. 77, 82, 86, 87, 138
Gittings, Kirk (Courtesy Syntax Photography); p.133
Hendricks, Paula; p. 100
Holf, Lindsay; p. 92
Lotz, Herb; p. 139, 147
Martinez, Maida; p. 23
McDermott, Michael; p. 152
Nohl, Mark (Courtesy *New Mexico* magazine); p. 11, 18, 50, 52, 54, 55, 150, 152, 153
Nussbaum, Jesse L.; p. 74, 76, 79
O'Connor, Paul; p. 57, 59
Parkhurst, T. Harmon; p. 17
Pollard, Pat; p. 59
Reck, Robert; p. 28, 39, 112, 117, 125, 126, 130
Studio Seven Productions; p. 37
Wironen, Norman; p. 96

With Special thanks to the Museum of New Mexico, Southwest Spanish Craftsmen, and the Heard Museum for the permission to reprint photographs.